Praise for *The Santa Story Revisited*

"*The Santa Story Revisited* is just plain delightful. I recommend it to the child in every one of us who still believes. This book is a service to mankind!"
> —**Christiane Northrup, M.D.**, ob/gyn, physician and author of the New York Times bestsellers: *Women's Bodies, Women's Wisdom* and *The Wisdom of Menopause*

"Truth, honesty, and integrity are essential messages we give our children. THE SANTA STORY REVISITED is a marvelous way of honoring the magic of Santa without deception. This is parenting at its best."
> —**Larry Dossey, M.D.**, author of *The Power of Premonitions* and *Healing Words*

"What an amazing new view of the Santa story we have lived as children and adults! This work is transformative—a positive shift in consciousness for kids and parents in a fun and easy manner. Without leaving good old Santa behind, readers and listeners are lifted to understand Santa as a living metaphor for love, compassion, kindness and generosity for all, every day of the year. This is a wonderful way to move our children (and us) from a December 25th awareness of 'me' to a year-round consciousness of 'we.' Our world is a much better place because of this beautiful book."
> —**Tom Zender**, President Emeritus of Unity

"Life is a series of allegories that teach us the illusions of life. Just as the stories of *The Little Red Hen* and *Peter Rabbit* are archetypal myths, the Santa metaphor provides one of life's basic messages—that our single greatest instinct is to nurture others. THE SANTA STORY REVISITED emphasizes the metaphorical essential of giving and nurturing—ultimately the true meaning of Love—the desire to do good to others. The Santa archetype is alive and well in the many good actions of humans. On a personal note, Santa is such an important archetype for me that I began collecting Santas from

around the world about 15 years ago. My collection has grown so much that I have had to alternate my Santas each year, displaying only half at a time. My grandchildren cherish these monuments to giving/nurturing just as much as I do. ' "The time has come," the Walrus said, "to talk of many things." ' Now is the time to talk about the REAL meaning of THE SANTA STORY."
—**C. Norman Shealy, M.D., Ph.D.**, author of
Pony Wisdom for the Soul and 25 other books

"Every parent should take note of Arita Trahan's feat. She has crafted a creative and insightful way to deal with one of the most beautiful and yet most challenging issues affecting parents—how to present Santa Claus without losing credibility when the inevitable occurs, the dreaded moment when the myth is debunked. Not only does Ms. Trahan offer an inspiring and novel method of presenting the Santa story, but she also deftly coaches the reader through many possible scenarios of dealing with questions and situations that may occur in the process. Drawing upon a child's innate and wondrous sense of play and imagination, she crafts a Santa for the 21st Century and beyond, one that maintains all the magic and joy, but one that also preserves and even strengthens the most basic and sacred bond of trust between parent and child."
—**Rick Seay, Ed.D.**, Academic Dean,
Montgomery Bell Academy

"This wonderful little book introduces a whole new 'enlightened' paradigm regarding Santa, allowing all of us to transcend our childhood disappointment regarding the 'jolly old elf.' Arita Trahan's retelling of Santa by expanding the story will delight kids—and parents no longer have to deal with the inevitable disenchantment and distress that ensues when their children would otherwise hear that Santa is not real."
—**Leslie M. Andrew, MS, BCET,**
Educational Therapist

"Arita Trahan has done something truly WONDERFUL with her Santa story! By introducing Santa as an intimate family game that is based on giving—not consumption or receiving—she has preserved what is best about Santa, while expanding the fun. With Arita's approach, Santa lives in our hearts, and he becomes actual in our imaginations whenever we want him to be, that being whenever we play the game. I love the honest nature of her thinking here. *The Santa Story Revisited* will be highly enlightening to parents, grandparents, in short...EVERYONE."

        —**Arlan Godthaab**, Actor (sometimes Santa)

"In *The Santa Story Revisited*, Arita Trahan shares ways to use the child's innate use of fantasy and gift of imagination as an expanded way of enjoying Santa more. This is wisdom for all year round, not just Christmas. For the child you love and the inner child that you are, it offers a sensitive and generous way to approach the Santa story."

        —**Candy Paull**, author of *The Most Wonderful Time of the Year* and *The Art of Abundance*

"What I like most about *The Santa Story Revisited* is the way Arita expands Santa into a game that emphasizes the joy of giving. It is a practical way to encourage each child to participate in Santa-like acts of kindness. This book is a refreshing approach to Christmas, given the ever-increasing commercialism of this wondrous holiday. This is a Santa every parent can feel happy about sharing with their little ones."

        —**Lance Hoppen** of the band Orleans

"This delightful book presents a new way to teach generosity, love, industry and kindness to children. It helps parents become conscious of their intention in story-telling while also encouraging children to see Santa as a hero they can emulate."

        —**Giuditta Tornetta**, author of *Painless Childbirth*

"*The Santa Story Revisited* has revitalized my enthusiasm for Santa and playing my own role in the Santa game, with a sense of inclusion and playfulness. Arita Trahan's book gives us a common foundation for celebrating during the holidays. While still maintaining our own personal faith-based beliefs, we can enjoy Santa as mentor of generosity, the impetus behind small gifts and acts of kindness."

        —**Andrea Sholer, MA**, Spiritual Psychology

The Santa Story
REVISITED

How to Give Your Children a Santa
They Will Never Outgrow

Arita Trahan
with Norma Eckroate

down **S** tream
enterprises

Published by Downstream Enterprises LLC
10815 Hesby Street, Suite 103
North Hollywood, CA 91601

ISBN 10: 0-9825328-0-6
ISBN 13: 978-0-9825328-0-5
UPC: 853361002011

Library of Congress Control Number: 2009935223

Publisher's Cataloging-in-Publication
Trahan, Arita.
    The Santa story revisited : how to give your children
a Santa they will never outgrow / Arita Trahan with
Norma Eckroate.
       p. cm.
      1. Santa Claus. 2. Child rearing. 3. Generosity.
      4. Maturation (Psychology)   I. Eckroate, Norma,
1951-
II. Title.
GT4992.T73 2009   394.2663
                         QBI09-600141

Printed in the United States of America.

15 14 13 12 11 10 9 8 7 6 5 4 3 2 1

Cover Design by Francis Sporer

This book is available at quantity discounts for bulk purchases.
For information, please call 818-392-0400

www.TheSantaStory.com

For Jaie and Alexa,
who taught me how to play Santa

CONTENTS

ACKNOWLEDGEMENTS

To Dennis Wile, whose frequent response to me was "Have you written that down?"

To my parents, Ruth and Andy, and my brother, David—the perfect family for me.

To Norma Eckroate, for being the impetus and the ballast in this writing adventure, for her kinder voice and steady faith.

To Sheila Cowan, who told me that to live a full life one must have a child, plant a tree, and write a book.

To Mark Horwitz, for moving into this adventure (literally) and filling my sails with music and laughter.

To my fourth-grade teacher, Mr. Smith, who heard my voice and gave it a platform.

To Cayman Grant and Kim Russell, for the invitation to play in their bright light and Cayman's directive to "Have fun with it."

To Holly Butler, who celebrates with me.

To Michael Bernard Beckwith, for surprising me into the awakening of what I always knew.

To Esther and Jerry Hicks, who taught me to enjoy the ride downstream.

To Andrea Sholer, Paul Owens, and Leslie Andrew, for their thoughtful input and fabulous editing suggestions.

To The Nashville Center for Spiritual Living, Agape International Spiritual Center, and The NoHo Center for New Thought, for their fertile community environments.

To the many people who generously revealed their Santa stories to us as we researched this book.

To Steve Trinward, for the fine filter of his copyediting skills.

To Francis Sporer, for his vision and creativity in so beautifully expressing our vision with his magnificent cover art.

To Meryl Ann Butler, for her patience and tireless devotion to detail in laying out the book so beautifully and for putting her masterful creative energy into each and every page.

—A.T.

I join Arita with heartfelt thanks to all of those who contributed to this book—and to Michael Bernard Beckwith, the Agape community, and Esther and Jerry Hicks, all of whom inspire my life!

In addition, I especially thank:

My goddaughter, Joie-May Silvers, who inspires and delights me.

Arita, for the joyous adventure down the river as we created this book. Yes, Arita, there is a Santa Claus. Thanks for bringing the expanded Santa into my life! Thanks, too, for the song *I'm Being Santa*. Your lyrics and Mark's music bring everyone's "inner Santa" to life. I can't get that song out of my head!

My parents, Alice and Vince, who joyously played Santa for me and my sister, Janet (Mari).

The many friends and relatives who are so lovingly supportive, with a special call-out to the Monday night study group: Meryl Ann Butler, Ariana Weil and Torsten Voges, Arita Trahan and Mark Horwitz, Constance Hall, Tony Romanov, Margaret Laspino, Eric Johnson, Evie Moore, Jeannette Namkung, Jeff Keasberry, Wendy and John Silvers, Leslie Andrew, Melissa Knight, Rich Yaker, and Archie Tulles. You light up my life!

—N.E.

DEDICATED TO SANTAS EVERYWHERE

WHO IS SANTA?

Santa is a giver of gifts.

Santa is selfless.

Santa never complains or asks for anything in return.

Santa is tireless.

Santa is faithful.

Santa is a worker of magic, a shape-shifter, and a time-bender.

Santa's deeply resonating "ho-ho-ho" is the epitome of joy!

How Can a New Santa Story Serve Us?

For the religious, Santa is a saint modeled on the generosity and compassion of Saint Nicholas and an expression of unconditional love, gifts of grace, and miraculous abundance.

For the non-religious, Santa represents no doctrine, other than love and generosity.

For the lonely, Santa is the stranger/friend.

For the tired, Santa comes while you are resting.

For the sad, Santa's joyful countenance accompanies every visit.

For the poor, Santa's gifts are given freely and without condition.

For the aimless, Santa demonstrates a joyful life purpose expressed through giving!

Santa can belong to anyone and everyone. Santa is a story that springs from ancient times and is ever evolving. In the pages of this book, you'll find a Santa that can be adapted in any way you'd like and played as a game by all ages.

INTRODUCTION

What if we could appreciate Santa more and enjoy Santa longer? What if Santa needn't ever be outgrown? What if playing with Santa was pure fantasy without even the tiniest bit of "deception" that might later diminish the experience?

Each year, parents are faced with a dilemma—how can we continue to keep *the secret* so our children can continue *to believe* in Santa? When they are very young it seems so simple. But with each passing year, our hold on the "believing in" part becomes more tenuous. As you'll discover in these pages, as a child, I took it pretty hard when the older kids told me that Santa wasn't real. I wondered how many other things my parents had said might not be true. Certainly such innocent woundings are simply a part of our growing up, but must Santa's delightful story be tarnished with memories such as mine?

In addition to keeping the secret, some parents are also challenged by other aspects of the Santa experience, like concerns about the role Santa should play in a religious holiday and the commercialization that sometimes seems to make the holidays more about the latest fad toy or how many goodies they can get from Santa, than about the spirit of giving. If you think about it, the only task that most of us give our children during this magical time is to make a list of all the stuff they want Santa to bring.

When I was a young mother, I longed for a more stable and expansive Santa experience for my children than the one I had. I wanted to give them a Santa that would be honest and magical and timeless. I wanted them to have a Santa that would enhance their lives and involve them in the story, giving them much more to do than simply making a list.

I came to the idea for the enhanced Santa that I share in this book one day when my older daughter was three. The spontaneous idea that unfolded was surprisingly simple. At the same time, it was so encompassing that it threatened no one and included everyone in its delightful invitation to play. It worked perfectly for me and for my family because it allowed Santa to morph into *more*—more fun, more creativity, and more opportunities to express the true meaning of the holiday he represents. If you choose, this is a Santa that can work for you, too.

The Santa story that I present in these pages offers you and your children so very much more than the one that most of us grew up with. If this new Santa story is a revolutionary idea, it is a quiet revolution. As you'll see, the generous nature of Santa that encompasses everyone in his bountiful giving can easily segue to encompass everyone as a game. Anyone who wishes can play—no matter our age. Any time someone engages in the story of Santa by simply talking about him, we are all invited to play along.

Because of the expansive nature of this Santa Story, it can be played openly without bringing the current construct of Santa into question. Children who learn this new expanded version of Santa can easily play alongside other children who still "believe in" Santa, without putting anyone's belief at risk.

You see, no one knew that my children were enjoying Santa in a different way. My children didn't even know it. They "behaved" much like other children during the holidays. They talked about Santa, wrote letters to Santa, planned for Santa's visit, elaborated on the stories they heard about him, read the books, and watched the movies. The only difference that a diligent observer might have noticed about my children and Santa was their emphasis on *both* giving and receiving.

Later in the book I offer some brief sample scripts that will help you easily segue to this new, expanded Santa. Some are for very young children who are first being told the Santa story; others are for children who have been playing Santa for a number of years. These scripts are simply a jumping-off point;

once you get the idea, you'll be able to carry forth with your own variations on the theme that are uniquely yours. And you may also want to check my website, *www.TheSantaStory.com*, for additional ideas submitted by other parents as they contribute their own magical ideas and stories of the ongoing experience that is Santa.

And, for those who are still conflicted about their own childhood experiences with Santa, Chapter 6, "The Ghosts of Santas Past," and Chapter 7, "Santa as a Rite of Passage," will be helpful.

Here's what *The Santa Story Revisited* does:

- It acknowledges Santa as the hero of anonymous giving and as a mentor for our own acts of generosity during the holidays and even beyond.

- It gives parents a Santa option that does not have a shelf-life, but instead cycles throughout the seasons of our lives without the need for any awkward adjustments.

- It liberates parents and their children into the *fantasy* of celebrating Santa without the limitations that *reality* can impinge on our hero.

- It invites adults to participate with their children in the expanded playfulness of the new Santa experience.

- It empowers parents as storytellers to inform and inspire their children.

- It assures parents that this new Santa experience does not threaten any other idea of Santa that may exist alongside it, but instead elaborates on the magic of Santa for everyone.

- It helps parents guide their children through any challenging segue from the believing-in stage.

- It assists adults in valuing their own Santa experiences as children—no matter how it might have unfolded.

- It presents the parent/child experience of Santa as a rite of passage, an archetype along the lines of *Pinocchio* and *The Wizard of Oz*.

- It creates a model for celebrating Santa that is less like a *religion of believing* and more like a *game for playing*—a modality more often demonstrated to adults by their children.

- It encourages parents to freely create and recreate new family traditions for themselves.

If your own Santa experience is already working for you, then perhaps there's no reason to change the way you are now celebrating the jolly gift-giver. However, if you find the ideas in this book compelling, please feel free to shape them to your own liking, take them to the next level, and increase your own Santa joy each season.

If you're like me, you love Santa and you want to enjoy the magic of his story year after year, with your children, grandchildren, the children of your friends and family, and your community in a way that is pure and easy and playful. Perhaps you, too, have wished for a way to embrace the Santa magic with greater honesty—a way that could not be "spoiled" by an overheard comment or the discovery of a well-hidden present. Welcome to a new Santa for a new generation.

If you want to cut to the chase and find my suggestions for segueing to the new Santa, you may skip ahead to Chapter 4.

CHAPTER 1

MY SANTA STORY
FROM THERE TO HERE

On the surface, my childhood experience with Santa looked like your typical Hallmark image. Most children in the same situation would have had a ball. All the elements for success were in place. I was the first child of a middle class family, with loving, doting parents in the 1950s. It was an era of aluminum trees and revolving color wheel lights, talking dolls, and electric trains.

I just loved reading *The Night Before Christmas* and had even learned it by heart. I also remember especially loving a book about Santa and a little girl who wrote to him asking for a toy dog. In the book, Santa's very own friendly dog named Jingles had a litter of pups. Santa was enjoying the frisky puppies at play, when he had an inspired idea. He tucked the black spotted puppy (who looked just like Jingles) inside his warm red coat. The next morning the little girl found the pup asleep inside her big Christmas stocking. Imagine getting something even better than you asked for!

MY PARENTS' CONSTRUCT OF SANTA

I loved everything about Santa. Well, *almost* everything. I always felt uncomfortable and sad when I saw Santa ringing that bell on the sidewalk, bored and tired and begging for a handout, or sitting in that stinky-smelling suit in the store. The image of him in the books and in my mind was just so much more delightful.

And then there were the visits with Santa when he sat in that giant chair at the department store. I've always been introspective, so there was no stopping my quiet deliberation that something about Santa just didn't seem right. I recall watching a mother proudly hand her sweet baby girl over to Santa and the wary expression on the infant's face as she looked up into that massive beard. There was a moment of silence, and then an ear-splitting wail. The tense embarrassing bundle with her screwed up red face was quickly passed back to the disappointed mother, as Santa moved on down the long line of kids, their endless lists of toys and parents eager for a photograph.

My friend Tony recalls sitting on Santa's lap as a small child and smelling such nasty bad breath that he leaned in and bit Santa on the nose. I was too big to squall and biting wasn't my style, so I just stood there, serious, off to the side, watching everyone else climb on board the Santa idea. And because I felt skeptical, I also felt guilt.

You see, the way I understood it, questioning belief was a sin, and boy, did I have questions: Why doesn't Santa gift-wrap my presents like he does for everyone else? Why doesn't he look the same as the Santa we saw last week? How does he get in the house when we don't have a chimney? And why won't you let me tell him that all I really want is a pony? Every question was met with a disapproving look and the quiet insistence that I "just believe." I had heard that same admonition many times before at church and, because I was a good girl, I tried to heed it. Since "faith is blind," I told myself, "Just believe—and don't look on the top shelf of the closets."

I ask your indulgence as I delve into the high drama of this tale. I assure you that although the focus of my adult years has shifted well toward taking life much more lightly, the factual telling of my youthful adventure with Santa must be as grand as any fairytale with witches and princesses, for so it felt to me at the time. I think back on it now with great fondness, for if I hadn't stumbled in my own dance with Santa, it is very likely that I would not have had the exciting discoveries revealed in these chapters.

My school photo at age 8, the year of my
personal "Santa rite of passage."

On that fateful day at school when the big kids taunted me
and my friends at recess, telling us that Santa wasn't real, I
covered my ears and tried hard not to hear. When they
chorused insistently, I screamed at them, "*My* parents wouldn't
lie to me. My parents *never* lie!!!!" I couldn't wait to get home
and tell my mom what had happened. But when I did, she was
oddly silent. I stood frozen with shock. After a moment of that
awkward, telling silence she simply said, "Those kids are up to
no good." I had wanted more. I had wanted her to tell me that
they were lying. As I stood there, feeling the foundation of my
beliefs falling away, I chose to pretend that nothing had
changed. I asked no more questions about Santa that day—or

ever. I sensed that my "believing" was important to my parents. And the more they seem pleased with my little-girl naiveté, the more I feared that they might not find a bigger, less naïve me quite as lovable.

Shortly after that day, my parents asked me if I still believed in Santa. I felt an immediate panic that they might see the truth in my eyes, but I said, "Yes." This is the first time I remember telling my parents a lie. The realization that they had not been honest with me had proved a turning point in our relationship; discussing the issue with them didn't seem to be an option. I had thought my parents were my "safe place," but somehow we'd crossed a threshold. I stepped back from them emotionally and, from that point, I felt that I could no longer fully believe anything they told me.

In my world, telling the truth was very important. I vividly recall an incident involving my favorite teacher, Mr. Smith, that stands out as one of great significance in my childhood. I had discovered that one of the metal arms on my school desk had become loose, and my friend and I figured that I could use it to tap out "secret signals" to her during class.

Later that day, when we were all quietly working on an assignment, I decided to try it out. I "sent" one of these signals and watched for her response. But she didn't seem to hear it, so I tapped again. She didn't even look up. Why wasn't she responding? Suddenly I heard Mr. Smith say from right behind me, "Are you trying to get someone's attention?" I jumped guiltily in my seat as "No!" sprang from my lips. What had happened? I hadn't planned to tell a lie, but there it was.

The realization of what I had done caused me to blush and burn with shame. I can still remember the way it physically hurt in the core of my little body. I cannot imagine Mr. Smith ever scolding anyone, and certainly not me, had I simply been honest with him. But it was too late. I was caught—without the courage to extract myself from my wrong-doing. Of course, there was also the embarrassment that came from having done something so dumb! Mr. Smith thought I was smart, so how could I confess to being so stupid? I suspect that guilt and embarrassment might be frequent companions.

I thought I was incapable of lying. And I was wrong. I found myself disappointed with the situation on all sides. I had taken my parents and our religious community seriously when they taught me that I should live each day without sin. So, the realization that those same grownups had been dishonest in what they told me about Santa seemed bigger than I was equipped to handle. Such is the stuff of which childhood drama is made.

With the passing of time, the weight of my own Santa pretense with my parents became too heavy to bear. They didn't ask me anymore if I still "believed in" Santa. Apparently they didn't want to know. What if I had to lie forever? So I fortified myself and walked into the kitchen to tell my mom the truth.

In that important moment of confession there was no upset and no discussion. I said whatever it was that I said, as simply and quickly as I could. I no longer remember exactly what it was, but I do remember that my mom responded by turning away from me and back to whatever she was doing in the kitchen. Thinking about it now, I suspect she was a bit embarrassed by the whole thing. For me, it felt as though I had lost her attention—like it suddenly became difficult for her to look me in the eye.

Suddenly, without any prior awareness that there were two sides to this story, I had crossed over to the other side of the equation. Where did I fit into the whole Santa story now? How would I answer strangers who asked what I wanted from Santa? My little brother still believed. So now it felt like it was my job to make sure he remained that way—to *protect* him from the truth. And the deceitful game continued, with me re-cast and playing a new role.

Acknowledging the truth and coming clean about my own deceit did not extricate me from collusion. I felt I was still expected to perform within the construct, not as an adult, and no longer as a child. It was an uncomfortable position in which I had become dangerous to the innocence of other "believers" and a disappointment to the perpetrators of the tale. I was enmeshed in the play but could not understand or appreciate the role in which I was now cast. I was simply "in the way." It was a problem to me as that little person. And the awkwardness extended well beyond the season for me since God and Santa seemed pretty much the same except for the red coat ... and the jolly part. If all of this Santa stuff wasn't real, I wondered what else was just a made-up story that would later be recanted?

I know now that my Santa experience was just that—MY experience. Why didn't I just relax and take everything more lightly? I don't know. I just didn't. My discomfort within this Santa experience didn't scar me for life, but it did inform me. It taught me that my parents didn't always tell the truth. It taught me that a big part of life is for me to determine how—and if—I fit in. It taught me to make choices for myself as to what and whom to believe and what to "believe in." And it definitely colored the experience I had later with my own children.

MY TURN TO PRESENT SANTA

Fast-forward to my own parenting: Santa was everywhere—a cultural event that swept everyone into its wake. Surely the spirit of the season, and of Santa himself, was worth redeeming, apart from a ritual of "believing in." I wondered if there were any options for parents. Couldn't fantasy be enjoyed as fantasy, without a lingering sense of deception or betrayal? I knew that I didn't want to just fall into the established plan. And I also knew that I didn't want to go to war with it.

Parenting is such an amazing assignment. All our aspirations are lined up to create a perfect world for the perfect beings that have been miraculously placed in our charge. All our intentions are to be wise and good and strong for them in ways we might have never been for ourselves. But, in our everyday reality, we aren't always secure about that wise, good, and strong stuff. If we are going to do anything other than follow old patterns, it seems we have no choice but to forge ahead into new situations and new demands, making it up as we go along. I marvel at the brilliance of the experience. It's improvisation at its best! I have found that even when I think I have a plan, the moment can never be exactly what I anticipated, and I often flounder. And there's nothing wrong in that. Often there is inspiration and, dare I say, even genius in the floundering. Looking back, I am glad to say that I have become a person who is more often comfortable in her floundering. While the situation might appear frighteningly raw, I frequently discover my wisest response by allowing loving intention and ignorance to be fully present at the same time.

When the day arrived that my three-year-old daughter Janine asked me to tell her about Santa, I felt myself begin to flounder, without a plan. I found myself listening to the response that spontaneously came out of my lips. It was amazingly simple: "Well, honey, Santa is a story—a really good story that everyone likes to tell. And more than that—Santa is a game that almost everyone likes to play. And it's all about giving gifts!"

There it was—a simple answer that I liked. The more the idea rolled around in my head, the more I could appreciate how gracefully encompassing it was. The concept of Santa had always seemed enormous. Now it seemed manageable and completely safe, too. As a game, it was innocent. Each person within it is free to play Santa however they were already playing, without judgment and without alteration. And others were free to join the game in their own way without complication or compromise. Inside this overarching concept there was room for every type of playing—without risk of undoing someone else's fun, and without the need to conform to another's beliefs.

Santa, whose whole story revolves around finding out what people want and then sneaking into their lives to surprise them with it, stepped forth simply as the hero who heralds the idea of giving anonymously. And Santa is so ho-ho-ho happy in his giving, that he never asks or expects anything in return. What a guy! And it's a game for children and grownups too. Visiting Santa and writing to Santa and talking about Santa are all a part of the game.

The next time a grown-up asked my little girl what she wanted Santa to bring her for Christmas, Janine looked over at me with a mischievous sparkle in her eye. She leaned close to his ear and brightly whispered her answer with a great deal of drama, boldly demonstrating to me her remarkable ability to play this Santa game very well.

Her grasp of the game became apparent in other ways too. Much to my surprise, I soon began to find oddly wrapped packages around the house. On the first of these occasions I remember musing aloud, "What's this?" Janine giggled and whispered, "It's from Santa!" As I opened the gift and said, "Who could possibly love me so much to surprise me with a present like that?" she pressed her little hands to her heart. Janine then slipped her arms quietly around my neck, her lips held tightly together, her Santa secret safe.

In those moments my daughter revealed another aspect of the Santa game that I hadn't considered. Since she often played the grownup with her dolls and stuffed animals, and enjoyed make-believe with a multitude of roles to play, she apparently saw no reason that anyone couldn't *play Santa—as Santa*. And so she did. My little child-Santa grew my heart that day and continues to do so every day that I recall her anonymous giving. Is there any better moment for a parent than to introduce a simple idea to her child and then be taught its fuller wisdom by that very child? Perhaps we can continue to benefit from the translations of our stories in the play of our children.

In our home, anonymous giving became synonymous with Santa on that day when this new construct of Santa revealed itself to my family. My daughter's new Santa story became my own new Santa story. By playing Santa *with* my children, instead of just *for* them, my children learned early to enjoy the giving as much as the getting.

If you were to ask my now-adult children about their Santa experiences, they would likely respond with quizzical expressions. That stand-apart moment was monumental for me since it was such a contrast with my own Santa experience, but it was not monumental for them. To them, it was simple and seamless. Santa was simply always there for them to play with and still is. The way they knew and enjoyed Santa never altered as they got older. It didn't need to as it was always expansive and imaginative and fun. Unlike their toys, they never outgrew Santa.

Later in this book, I share a children's story, titled simply *The Santa Story,* that focuses on *playing* Santa. Recently my younger daughter Alexa was reading it to a small group of her friends when one of them, Kelilah, suggested that perhaps growing up with this idea of Santa is the reason that Alexa is always so giving to others. How nice it is to hear that others perceive Alexa in this way.

The kindness and generosity of both of my daughters impresses everyone. I know of no more generous people on the planet than they. And, like the Santa they played as children, their giving is often in the form of acts of kindness. I suspect that the joy they experience in being such givers is something that the Santa game helped to mold very early in their lives. All I did was simply get out of the way and let their imaginations explore Santa, without any attempt to shape the story with a belief or an idea of what must appear as "real." In my opinion, my best work as a parent has been when I stepped back. Today I revel in all I *didn't* do that worked out so well.

PARENTING AND STORYTELLING

My biggest accomplishment as a mother was the joy that I felt when I was with my children. And I enjoyed the stories. Telling stories was a big part of our time together. It was a magical time of sharing and my girls loved to listen and participate. There were lots of stories in books, of course, but they also loved the stories that I told about friends and family, and the stories about what they were like when they were younger.

I love climbing in and out of the stories of other people's lives; doing so enriches and expands my own. Often I feel that I somehow become a part of whatever story I read or tell as if it were my own. I recall hours of sitting on the floor in the small hall that connected my daughters' bedrooms, reading to them as they lay in bed at night. I volunteered as the story-lady one day a week at their school, reading to classes from kindergarten through fourth grade. I remember vacationing with my parents and reading aloud to them. I read book after book after book aloud whenever I had the opportunity and an audience to listen. This was for my own pleasure as much as it was for them. To me, life is a collection of stories.

One of my favorite create-your-own storytellers is my photographer friend, Dennis Wile. Known for his distinctive commissioned portraits, Dennis disdains manufactured poses and is proud to say that he never asks anyone to smile. As he explains, "I never use the 'S' word." Instead, he captivates his subjects, no matter what their age, with the most amazing stories. Just as you think the story is going one way, it takes a turn and catches the listener off-guard. I worked with him for a couple of years and it was beautiful to witness his storytelling. His stories spark a magical response from his subjects that is visible in their portraits.

Dennis inspired me to engage more creatively in my conversations with children, both my own and others whose lives intersected mine. So instead of waiting until story-time to be imaginative, I would play along with them with whatever they were doing, add to their games, and even begin a new story in the middle of a regular activity.

When I began this new *modus operandi*, I had a brief moment of concern that they would not know when I was *playing* and when I wasn't. But it was never a problem. When I stepped out of a bath-time story of sailing ships and big fish with a comment about something else, such as a cautionary remark about the temperature of the water, it still had the effect of reality that I felt it required. I found that I could then slip right back into the story without having to delineate fact from fiction. (Perhaps the natural tone of my voice made this distinction clear without any special effort.)

Although my children did not need me to play along in order to be perfectly content in their own fantasies, I found that I benefited from the lightness of the play, and my own creativity expanded as a result. I chose to visit the child's world of fantasy more frequently.

To every imaginative being, and particularly to children, almost anything is possible. An idea may certainly begin in the *seemingly* impossible realm—and, as I consider this now, it seems that every creative idea *must* begin there. Ideas are not, however, expected to remain *impossible*. The imagination we develop as children needn't be outgrown. Exercising our imaginations in stories and games stretches our potential for invention and discovery and expands our world.

Events and ideas, conversations, relationships, and activities —everything in the world of a child serves as a seed in their imagination. And children are fertile ground for every seed impression that we make. If you want to know what seeds you have planted, watch them growing in the stories and playtime of your child: *"I'll be the mommy and you be the daddy"* or *"I'll be the teacher and you be my student,"* and instantly a game begins. Another child steps in with her own idea of a role and spontaneous interaction unfolds—with objectives and tasks and relationships. They are constantly organizing ideas and information in their play—playing as truthfully as they can. If any part doesn't seem "right," it is challenged or corrected or nudged in a different direction. The amount of wiggle-room in the imaginary situation depends on the child and what they perceive as true or possible. They practice discerning right and wrong, true and false, in this imaginary realm. They begin by reflecting in their playtime exactly what they have learned from their adults. They are actors in an adult play, trying on various roles and learning them from the inside out. As we observe them, they demonstrate to us what we as parents have taught them.

WHO IS SANTA?

My co-author Norma told me that one year she asked Santa for a bride doll. I remember the bride doll I had. She was beautiful, standing there on my dresser, not exactly the kind of dolly I would play with, but one I cherished. However, the bride doll Norma got from Santa wasn't like mine. Norma got a baby doll for which her mom had sewn a bride dress. Her mother must have schemed to find a way to satisfy Norma's wish, perhaps lacking the funds to do so in the normal way. But it didn't work. Norma remembers thinking, "Baby dolls don't wear bride dresses. This doll isn't from Santa. Santa knows what a bride doll looks like, and this isn't it!" And in that moment came the revelation—the revealing of mom and dad as Santa. The "bride" doll Norma received from well-intentioned parents was wrapped in disappointment and upset. But, like so many of us, Norma didn't want to disappoint her loving parents by letting them know that she knew that they were the providers of the gifts that were attributed to Santa. She knew far more

15

than her parents were aware of and carefully juggled truth and fiction in order to accommodate them in their pretense and herself in her knowing.

Another friend, Tony, had spent hours and hours as a child perusing the Sears Christmas catalog, circling all of the hoped-for toys, and folding down the corners of pages to make sure his choices were duly noted. To Tony, the Sears catalog that he was given each year to revel in was "Santa's catalog." He had a big moment of revelation one Christmas season as he accompanied his mom on a shopping trip to Sears.

Having learned enough of the alphabet to recognize the sign on the outside of the store and correlate it with the word "Sears" on the catalog cover, he surmised that Santa must work for Sears. He asked his parents if that was the case and they said yes. But when Christmas came and Tony wondered why Santa didn't give him what he asked for, his parents responded that, "Santa must have gotten it wrong." To Tony, it felt like they were making excuses. It finally all added up—and Tony no longer believed in Santa.

Perhaps a child's developing ability to deduce, to relate cause and effect, to sort fact and fiction, to decide if it's the right time to engage in an issue or not, all sorts itself out in the end with or without the participation of adults. Interestingly, when I talk to adults about their childhood experiences with Santa, almost all of them remember exactly how and when they came to the truth when they were children, even when their parents were not forthcoming about it. And yet, when they became parents themselves, they still expected their own children to continue to accept the Santa story they told as fact. Parental naiveté runs rampant.

SANTA AS STORY

Why do we talk of Santa anyway? What is the attraction? My own answer comes easily. He is only about giving. He plans and works and thinks about nothing else. All year he gathers and builds and stores away gifts for everyone. He plots to know all our secret wishes. He sneaks into our lives and leaves happy surprises. He asks for nothing in return. He is jolly even though he works constantly. And he endures cold and physically impossible feats.

There is no story of Santa receiving a gift that I have ever heard—other than cookies and milk to fortify him along his way. He basically travels alone, unless you count the reindeer, who have taken on some human-like emotions in recent decades. Santa has amazing powers that he uses toward a generous end. He loves us all without exception. Is there anything about Santa not to love? He is even happy with his body image! Is anyone else in your life as jolly as Santa—who laughs for no reason but joy?

I want to be Santa. Don't you?

CHAPTER 2

HARNESSING THE POWER OF STORYTELLING
STORIES PERSONAL AND FANCIFUL

Few stories have the scope of Santa. Celebrated for almost a month each year and rich in sensory impressions, Santa is a symbol that feeds our collective soul with goodness and cheer. It may be one of the most widely shared stories in the world, throughout many cultures and passed along from one generation to the next. Through music and imagery and shopping and foods, the telling of Santa's story permeates work, school, and family. Whether we actively or passively subscribe to this societal foray, Santa sweeps through our lives. We are caught in its wake and, as with any archetype, how we translate that energy is up to us. Yet, despite all the common denominators regarding the Santa story, there are numerous variations in the way the story has been told to us, as well as variations in the way each of us *understood* the story, and, as a result, the way it played out in our own childhood Santa experiences.

THE IMPRESSIONABLE YEARS

Stories are fundamental to life's journey; we are the product of the stories that we were told and the stories we continue to tell through our lives. The bottom line is that we are always at choice when it comes to our stories. When we tell stories to very small children, they believe them to be true and factual. Then, starting at about the age of seven, they begin to differentiate between what is fantasy and what is real.

When Christy was about 4, her mother, Meryl Ann, heard that it was good to introduce kids to real-life stories. She learned of a series of biographies written for children and bought one on Louis Pasteur. Sitting down to read it to Christy, she explained that this book was a biography and told her, "That means it's not like the other stories we read. This is a TRUE story about a real person who really lived and really did the things that we are going to read about in this book." Christy looked at her mother with big eyes and quivering lips and asked, "Momma, do you mean that all those other stories aren't true?" Meryl Ann flashed on the recent bedtime stories, *Runaway Bunny, Goodnight Moon, Velveteen Rabbit,* and *Where the Wild Things Are.* Suddenly she had a deeper insight into the magical world of her 4-year-old daughter and thought, "Of course, it's *all* real to her."

Me with my dolls on the front stoop of the playhouse my father built for me. Years later, my mother reminisced that I constantly talked to my dolls and told them what they could and could not do.

My mother always told me that as a child I played very seriously. Apparently it not only felt very real to me, but also very important. Besides Santa, my earliest memories of storytelling came from a few well-worn books that my parents read to me. Growing up, mine was not a house of many books, as it is now. There were the standard Mother Goose stories, as well as collected traditional tales like *Three Billy Goats Gruff* and Hans Christian Anderson. I still have my copy of an early favorite, *Just Like Mommy, Just Like Daddy*. The book perfectly represents the typical sexual stereotype most of us automatically embraced during the 1950s. Even the form of the book is indicative of its duality, as the *Mommy* story is read from one side of the jacket and the *Daddy* story from the flip side. The images of a mother and daughter moving through the tasks of their day, happy and content, looking forward to the end of the day when Daddy comes home, were very dear to me. It also described my life at home exactly. It was a sweet book and I understood my half of its gender-specific title as an edict for shaping my life. It was many years before it occurred to me that women could enjoy any of the tasks or games presented in the other half of the book. My life reflected the stories I was told.

I was a first generation TV child, entertained and informed by the stories of *Leave it to Beaver, Captain Kangaroo, Bonanza, Lassie, Superman, Davy Crockett* and *Roy Rogers*. Then came *Patty Duke, The Flying Nun* and *I Dream of Jeannie* (with her "Yes, Master"). It was an era of "men as men and women as girls." It was clear that working in the yard was man's work and making the bed and ironing was for us gals. As a tomboy, I wanted my turn at cutting the grass and wasn't allowed until I bought a home of my own.

Perhaps due to the lessons of *Little Red Riding Hood* and *Hansel and Gretel*, I was never tempted to wander far from home. The special magic of storytelling via full-length movies was an unusual treat in my family. I recall *Cinderella*, *Lady and the Tramp*, and *The Wizard of Oz*. *The Shaggy Dog* also stands out because, to me, it was a horror story. For years I was afraid to look in the bathroom mirror at night for fear I would see long hairs growing out of my face. Apparently I was easily frightened. I am told that my parents had to take me out of the theater during the witch scenes of *Sleeping Beauty*.

My house-playing activities included a miniature ironing board, complete with an iron that actually became warm when it was plugged in, and the infamous Easy Bake Oven. I played by hanging doll clothes on a low-hanging line and "painting" my swing set and the dog's house with a brush and pail of water. I was an easy child whose imagination stretched only as far as the yard around my house. My stories were my life in training-wheels and, truth be told, I enjoy ironing, baking, and decorating to this day.

Very young children accept the stories we tell them as "real" for a reason. Children are highly receptive to input from the world around them because Nature has set them up to thrive. In his book, *The Biology of Belief*, Dr. Bruce Lipton tells us that young children's brains develop in a way that allows them to access an incredible volume of information.

From birth to age two, the brain operates *predominately* at the lowest brainwave frequency of 0.5 to 4 cycles per second (Hz) (known as *delta* waves) and, from ages two until six, at a higher level of 4 to 8 cycles (known as *theta* waves). The highly

My younger brother and me. Note the white gloves I'm wearing in
this photo. On Sunday morning before church my Mother would
say, "You can go outside, but stay clean." It was an era of "men as
men and women as girls."

receptive, suggestible, and programmable state of *theta* is
sometimes called "hypnagogic," because it is similar to the
transitional state adults experience between wakefulness and
sleep. This hypnagogic state allows young children to "...

carefully observe their environment and download the worldly wisdom offered by parents directly into their subconscious memory. As a result, their parents' behavior and beliefs become their own."[1]

So what does this all mean? This hypnagogic state not only supports the nurturing of children so they can deal with the world outside of them, it also allows them to have rich fantasy lives.

> *I remember going to bed on Christmas Eve and my mother telling me to listen for Santa's sleigh bells, which meant he was getting near. And as I would lie there, focusing my ears on the sounds of the night, I could actually hear those bells. I reveled in the awareness that Santa was on his way.*
>
> *(Constance)*

In her beautiful story, "The Magic of Christmas" on *Mothering.com*, Bethany Rountree explains that she had always told her children that Santa wasn't a real person but was part of the spirit of Christmas. On the Christmas Eve when her middle child, Ethan, was five, he confirmed with his mother that Santa was not real. Then Ethan decided to write a letter to Santa anyway.

Later, when Ethan could not find the letter he'd written, he ran outside and, moments later, came back reporting that he had seen Rudolph leading a sleigh and that Santa was in the

---

[1] Lipton, Bruce H., Ph.D., *The Biology of Belief*, Hay House, 2005, page 132.

sleigh with a bagful of letters. Rountree was delighted and tells us, "He was off and running in his own world.... The truth about Santa Claus had not taken away my children's innocence."[2]

THE STORIES THAT WE BECOME

Flash-forward to the beginning of my adult experience—which looked just like my mother's. In this there was no surprise or disappointment; as a young woman, my first and only career choice was motherhood. I was as submissive and soft-spoken as Mrs. Cleaver, while my dreams of magical powers were more focused on impressing a man the way Jeannie did than expanding my own experience of life.

I played house with my children just as I had played dolls. The idea that my life would one day outgrow mothering was almost terrifying. It seemed that my life, in order to be purposeful, depended on having babies and raising them. I would lie awake at night wondering what I would do with myself when my children were grown—a miserable prospect for me at the time.

On reflection, it seemed as though I was prepared emotionally for nothing else. (In writing this I accidentally typed: "prepared emotionally for *nothing less*." Surely that was a

---

[2] "The Magic of Christmas" by Bethany Rountree; published on *www.Mothering. com*, accessed August 28, 2009.

Freudian slip, for I still believe there is no more important or fulfilling role to play in life than parenting.)

In modern life, we are exposed to countless stories—stories from books, TV and movies, stories from families and friends and teachers, bedtime stories and parables and proverbs, stories of where we came from and why we are here (both in the macrocosm and the microcosm), stories of what is and what might be. Some of them have profound impact on us and others are forgotten in short order.

The stories that impact us, consciously and/or subconsciously, likely hold the shape of our futures. They don't have to be the scale of *Gone With the Wind* or *Star Trek* to be important, although the level of emotion they evoke and the frequency with which they are re-told, re-read, or re-visited contribute to and indicate the measure of their impact in our lives.

What are the stories that define what you have become? The ones read to you or by you, the ones you saw again and again on the screen, or listened to over and over in a song? Has your attraction to romantic stories of unrequited love led you to unrequited loves of your own? Has your delight with stories of adventure pushed you over the edge more than once? Was your appetite for the imaginative or fantastic later revealed in a creative avenue?

Perhaps the story of your parents' lives has served as a template for yours. What were your foundational stories, especially during those impressionable years? When we become aware of the way certain stories have impacted our own lives, it can serve as impetus to offer a thoughtful array of stories to our children, like a buffet of ideas from which they can serve themselves outlines for the future. As you move through your day, consider what you do with your time and your mind, the surroundings you have chosen for life, work, and play. Was there an early influence in story form that echoes through your life?

REVEALING OUR ONGOING STORIES

On a surface level our personal stories are revealed regularly, both to ourselves and to each other. Even comments about the traffic and weather reveal the ways we embrace the cycles of life. We can't help but tell the world the story of what holds our attention, whether we intend to or not.

The other day, my husband drew my attention to a beautiful woman who was standing behind us in line at Costco. He was puzzled by the dark look of anger on her face, as she stood there alone in the crowd. "What could her story be?" he wondered aloud. We could see its dominant tone even without a clue as to the specifics.

As an actor, I hone my craft by studying the way people express themselves through their appearance, their body language, and their interactions with others. I often wonder about their stories. Have you ever played the game in an airport, either alone or with someone, in which you watch others in the crowd and imagine their relationship to the people they are with or the person they are talking to on the phone? You can guess where they are going and what kind of job they have. You can even guess what they are thinking. It is an interesting game to introduce to your children. It makes them more conscious of how much we can tell about others by simply observing them. These observational skills also alert them to the ways in which they are broadcasting information about themselves to the world, apart from the words they are using.

As I write this, I am reminded of the old adage, "You can't judge a book by its cover." Does this suggest that I should qualify my playful suggestion to "read" others by their appearance? My desire is certainly not to stereotype people or judge their choices. I reconsider: "You can't judge a book by its cover." Hmmm. Publishers do spend a good deal of time and professional know-how designing book covers, in an attempt to accurately represent the book's contents to potential readers.

As an actor and as a woman, I know that my clothes and physical presentation reflect my personality, character, and, often, my immediate mood. I'm sure there are always exceptions, but in my experience, when there seems to be a discrepancy between the body and the spoken words, the body is most frequently the more honest of the two.

Imagine a teen pouting, slumped into a chair, his body closed off to the world, as someone asks, "What's the matter?" With a bitter tone, he snaps back, "Nothing! I didn't say anything." Although he is speaking one idea with his choice of words, his body language is very clearly declaring something else.

Research has shown that the *words* we use account for only seven percent of what is actually communicated, while 55 percent of communication is based on what is seen (our physical appearance) and 38 percent on sound and intonation. These three areas of communication were labeled as verbal, visual, and vocal, in the UCLA study.[3]

In our front yard in Lake Charles, Louisiana: My brother David's body language clearly indicates that he is much happier as one of the men than he is with my mom and me.

For example, someone who is considered sarcastic, as demonstrated in a dry vocal intonation and wry facial expression, is actually communicating the opposite of what he says. We instinctively find ourselves aware of this. So ... if you think that you don't speak "body language," you are unaware

---

[3] 1981 study, "Silent Messages," conducted by Professor Albert Mehrabian of the Department of Psychology at the University of California, Los Angeles.

that you are constantly doing so. You have merely relegated it to instinct and may even call it that. The first language we understood as infants did not require us to understand the words. My new grandchild teaches me how little words mean in the way she communicates at this early stage in her life. She seems to absorb the sensations and emotions of whomever is closest to her. Her budding smile and laughter are triggered by the genuine joy of her parents as they delight in her, a little mirror of her world.

Consider the amazing way our companion animals respond to a simple change of tone. If I begin to sound at all agitated in a conversation, Jaco, the more sensitive of my two dogs, will get up and leave the room. Once I noticed how sensitive Jaco was to my energy, I started to acknowledge his retreat as an early indicator of my emotional direction. I also found that my pup has this reaction whether I am experiencing a personal upset or telling a story about someone else's upset.

I'm sure there is much to learn from this. As a young child, I remember being so upset when the wicked witch wished Sleeping Beauty dead that my mother had to take me out of the movie theatre. So isn't it interesting that my dog can have essentially the same type of reaction to the emotions that I express. Jaco's honest response—perhaps a self-protective mechanism on his part—gives me greater emotional awareness when my "dark story" turns him away, though I am far from wishing anyone dead. Even without direct intention, we can be sure that our stories are being read by others—including our animals—all the time.

Your story is about the way you feel in your skin, your mind, and your heart. It's about looking at your options and making choices—and telling a story that works for you. Perhaps you feel that your family or your community or your culture has already created a story so dominating and prevailing that you have no choice. The good news is that stories can be told a multitude of ways. And it is in the telling of the story that we each make our personal impression.

INTENTIONAL STORYTELLING

Let's take a well-known and well-established story and imagine how it might be told. *The Three Little Pigs* gives us a fitting example. There is the cast of characters—three little pigs, each of whom expresses and behaves differently from the others, even though they may look alike ... and the wolf. In its briefest telling, three pigs build houses for themselves using different materials: straw, sticks, and bricks. Then the hungry wolf appears, looking for dinner. When he is not invited in for an easy feast of pork, and finds the doors to all three houses locked, the wolf succeeds in blowing down the first two houses. In the kinder version of the story, these two pigs run to safety in the brick house of the third pig, which the wolf is unable to blow down. Some stories end there; others depict the wolf attempting to get in to eat the pigs by going down the chimney. There are a variety of tales as to his fate from that point.

Consider the variety of intention in telling the tale. One storyteller might use the story to warn of the dangers in a world that seeks to destroy us—to eat us alive. Another might use it to demonstrate the various ways that we can build our lives/homes/ideas/faith to make us stronger. One might teach that a certain level of industry and effort is necessary to be successful in life. A fourth might use it to point out the differences in people, and convey the message that within community we find strength and safety and we all benefit by caring for one another. After all, if the pig with the brick house hadn't provided a safe haven to his friends with the houses of straw and sticks, he might have been the one deemed to have made the *right* decision, since he had the foresight to build a sufficiently sturdy home. But, at the end of the story, he would have had no one with whom to dance the jig.

Some of you might have heard the "life is hard" tales told by a previous generation: *"When I was young we had to walk five miles to school in the snow!"* This theme has often been elaborated upon and adapted, in an attempt to elicit gratitude from children who complain that going to school is a hardship. Imagine a small thin child dealing with slippery ice and a heavy load to bear. His clothes are inadequate for the weather, his skin painful with the cold. The road is long and lonely, and there is no happy ending. *"Poor Grandpa."*

Now imagine Grandpa telling the same story, but with a different slant. Add a clever way to strap the bundle on the back and make it manageable. Add layers of clothes— perhaps odd-looking, but warm and practical. Then imagine a rendezvous with a friendly neighboring dog, a jog to stay warm, and maybe a playful snowball fight with a friend. When Grandpa tells this version of the story, the grandchild's reaction could very well be, *"Why can't I walk to school in the snow?"*

Are you beginning to get the idea that it's really all in the way we tell the story that makes the difference? Stories have a reason as well as a season. Parables and tales have been used throughout time to explain and to instruct, to inspire and to warn. Why are you telling your stories? Why are others telling theirs to you? When we ask ourselves these questions, we are better tellers and better listeners. We are more intentional in the telling and more discerning and aware in the hearing.

I remember going to see a movie with friends who didn't like the way the story ended. They told me afterwards that they had re-written the ending to suit them. I remember thinking at the time, "Is that allowed?" and then laughing to myself at the idea of the *story police* rushing in to make an arrest. Why not welcome into our lives only the stories, and the endings, that we enjoy? In recent years, the stories presented in films have become more malleable as some films are released on DVD in special "director's cuts." Additional scenes and plot-points are not uncommon, telling a somewhat different story from the original release. So, which version of the story is the real one? Audiences are asked to accept this foray into creative expression and even celebrate the fact that there are different versions.

In most stories, including Santa's, there is the potential for disappointment, sadness, and fear. Any story about life contains all the possibilities of life. The stories and the telling of them teach us our options. I imagine it was someone who was concerned about Santa being alone that first came up with the concept of a Mrs. Claus. Someone else, who worried that this most beneficent being was never the recipient of a gift, thought up the milk and cookies offering. Another, concerned about challenging weather conditions, thought up Rudolph and his red nose as a youthful and transformational hero. Without them, the story of a lone soul traveling the planet on a cold night and a nearly impossible task could make a listener sad. Thank goodness for the raucous "ho-ho-ho" that is Santa's only commentary on life. It's all about joy.

And yet, there are those who tell stories to frighten others into obedience or submission, some even using Santa to this end. Apart from the season, telling stories to frighten and control has been done on a larger scale by institutions and also by cultures around the world for centuries. Consider those pigs again. The story is fraught with implications of laziness, carelessness, and the threat of a bloody death. There are corporations as well as individuals that might want us to think that a straw bale home or even one built of locally harvested sustainable timber could be weak choices in a dangerous world. Perhaps those first two pigs actually deserved to die! If this is a story for children, perhaps we should ban the book!

Or we could simply tell the story differently: *"There was once a pig who loved working with bricks. He didn't mind that it took longer, because he enjoyed the process and took pride in what he was doing."*

In this new rendition of the tale, perhaps the first two pigs simply were not keen on building, as was evident in their choice of building materials and their workmanship. Maybe the other two little pigs made fun of the brick-laying pig and called him names. Perhaps they were friends who sometimes disagreed about what was important. Nevertheless, there was one thing that all three pigs could agree on and loved to do together—and that was dancing the jig. Let the wolf move on to a different dinner. Dance a jig with your child. All is well.

FEELING OUR STORYTELLING

There are many different ways to tell the truth in our stories. I can tell the story of driving to work and mention only the number of cars on the road. Or I can tell about the exact same drive to work and speak only of the music I heard as I drove along, or how the heavy sweet fragrance of jasmine managed to permeate the traffic and my closed windows along the way. These are both stories of the same event and both can be called factual. One needn't choose between them in order to know what was true. They are both true. What is different is how they *feel*. They don't just tell two different truths about my ride, but two different truths about me. Which is my story? The most immediate indicator of the quality of my stories is how they feel.

What are the stories that we tell the most often and how do they *feel* to us and to our most impressionable audience, our children? What is the dominant tone of our stories as adults moving through our days? Children provide a magnificent audience; they give us a wonderful opportunity to see ourselves reflected in the stories we tell. And I don't mean just the ones that begin with "When I was your age…" or "This is what happened today." I'm talking about the stories that are implicit in every remark that we make. The comment to "hurry up" tells a story of impatience, or being the first one ready, or needing help with getting ready, or fear of lateness, or lack of time. It could also tell the story of excitement or an eagerness to begin.

Listen to yourself and hear your story. Become more sensitive to feeling your story. If it is a consistently good feeling story, then you can be sure that the story being shared with those around you is an offering of "feel good" to them as well. Although we can think our story is about *circumstances*, it is really more about *our response* to circumstances. It is the example we set for our children that teaches them far more than words ever could.

Imagine the way a new day might begin in your home. The moment you step from your bed there is a dominant feeling in your body that is your story. Regardless of what it is—tired or enthusiastic, reluctant or eager—your emotional tone provides the set-point for your story. Additionally, each individual in your home brings their own story to the table (pun intended) in the morning. We aren't bound to be affected by each other's stories and yet we often are. It is an option, just as every circumstance before us in each moment gives us a new option for storytelling. We are always writing our stories of the day. We can't write someone else's story, but we can invite them into ours.

Initially you might be more aware of the stories of those around you than you are about your own. As parents we can feel obliged to tell our children what is right or wrong about their behavior, as well as what is right or wrong about their appearance. But constantly judging anyone—ourselves, or others—is an exhausting job. It's annoying and disempowering to the recipient and to those who overhear it. Would we want to switch roles and constantly hear what our children consider our own poor choices? (If that has already happened to you, you have my sympathy.)

By focusing our attention on our own internal experience, we are less likely to become occupied in judging others. We are less likely to react to the behaviors around us that we don't care for, and much more likely to discover what feels good and allow ourselves to be drawn to that. When we do this, our story becomes more fun for us and, at the same time, it's definitely more fun for those around us. Our stories are then much more likely to yield a positive influence and we are empowered in the telling of them.

If I awaken feeling out of sorts for any reason, I can remind myself that it is simply a story, my story. If I don't like it, I can change it. In each moment there is choice of thought —the opportunity to focus upon something that either pleases or doesn't please. I am fascinated by the terrain of this journey. My business becomes taking care of myself. When I find myself derailed by circumstance or upset, I can still choose. I can think about how I feel, acknowledge that I want to feel better, and look around for a thought that *will* feel better. Sometimes the *better* thought might not look exactly cheery. But if it makes me feel even a bit better … well, that's still better. Better is better.

Here's the *best* part of this story. Happy people spread happiness and a positive attitude. Those around us feel that emotional set-point—and they then have the choice of joining in or not. In his book, *Social Intelligence: The New Science of Human Relationships*, Daniel Goleman talks about our mirror neuron systems and "… what scientists call a mutually reverberating state of 'empathetic resonance.' These systems allow us to grasp the mind of others not through conceptual reasoning but through direct simulation; by feeling, not by thinking."[4] It's just one more reason to spend time with people whose neurons we want to mirror, right?

I also find that when I am focused on feeling better, the people and the events around me conspire to support my choices to feel better. With our beloved children this is the best lesson possible. And what good news it is that we care best for them when we are caring best for ourselves.

What do I want my children to say about me?

"My mom likes everything done her way." or *"My mom goes with the flow."*

"My mom worries when …" or *"My mom sings around the house."*

"My mom gets upset when …" or *"My mom is the happiest person I know."*

You get the idea. Now back to Santa.

Whether your childhood experiences with Santa were happy or sad or something in between, the story you tell your children about these experiences might become the stuff of folklore. Santa did not visit my dad's house when he was a child. Dad remembers only one Christmas present—a big candy cane

---

[4] Goleman, Daniel, *Social Intelligence: The New Science of Human Relationships*, 2006, Bantam-Dell, New York, NY., page 43.

given to him by the Santa at the local movie theater. He thought that it was grand. He marveled at how big it was and how long it lasted. My dad's story of Santa and his life story are similar. He found ways to celebrate joy in the moment, appreciated the rich experiences of his past, and continually expressed gratitude for all the good things that unfolded in his life.

My mother's childhood Santa history was quite different. She told the story of hanging a stocking on the mantle each year despite the fact that her parents discouraged her from doing so. And, on each re-telling, she keenly reiterated the pain of always finding the stocking empty on Christmas morning— except for one year when, to her great delight, she found a small pocket-knife in the stocking. She later learned that her brother had placed it there to surprise her. Sometime after that, she was distressed when the pocket-knife went missing. Year after year, I remember hearing the story. Despite all of the years that had intervened, she continued to be upset about what might have happened to the missing knife.

Which dominant emotion is the backbone of your story— the story that your children will tell of you? And what is it that we find remarkable about Santa? What is the Santa story we tell our children when they are very young?

SANTA'S ROOTS

History demonstrates a tradition of Santa storytelling that is constantly morphing. It grabs an image here, and an idea there, and then the color of his coat changes from green to red. Our modern celebration of the Santa story goes back only a few generations: Santas appearing simultaneously on a myriad of street corners and at multiple malls, letters to Santa, pictures with Santa, Santa at the helm of a full-fledged toy factory, the quantity and extravagance of gifts that children receive ... all are mostly post-World War II additions to the tale.

Tracing his roots, the primary inspiration for today's Santa is Saint Nicholas of Myra, a fourth century Greek Christian bishop, who was famous for his generous, and frequently anonymous, gifts to the poor. (By the way, *Santa* is a derivative of *Saint* and *Claus* is a derivative of *Nicholas*.)

In Germanic folklore the story is even older. Parallels can be drawn to Odin, a pre-Christian god—depicted with a long white beard and spear (or staff)—who led a great hunting party through the sky during the holiday of Yule. Children put carrots, straw or sugar in their boots and placed them near the chimney as treats for Sleipnir, Odin's eight-legged flying horse who could leap great distances. In return, Odin rewarded the children with gifts and candy. After Christianity took hold in that part of the world, this practice was associated with Saint Nicholas.

In The Netherlands and some other countries, the primary day for gift-giving is December 6, the feast day of Saint Nicolas, who is known there as *Sinterklaas* or The Friendly Saint. He is assisted by helpers who are known as Black Peter (*Zwarte Piet*), inspired by the story that Saint Nicolas liberated a slave boy from Ethiopia, whose name was *Piter* (or Peter). There was originally only one Black Peter, but in post-World

War II Holland, the liberating Canadians thought that multiple Black Peters would be even more fun, so they added that twist to the tradition. (Though some consider the Black Peter story to be racist, today his skin color is no longer attributed to the race of the real-life boy who inspired the story, but rather to the soot in the chimneys that he climbs through.)

Elves plopped themselves into the Santa story in Scandinavia in the 1840s, when an elf called *Tomte* or *Nisse* began delivering the Christmas presents. Based on Nordic folklore, the newer version of this elf was portrayed as short and bearded, with gray clothes and a red hat.

Santa's fur-lined robe comes along in 17th Century Britain, when religious and folklore traditions merged into the character known as Father Christmas. He is pictured as well-nourished and bearded, with a long green, fur-lined robe.

In America, elements of both the British and the Dutch characters merged into Santa Claus. As I mentioned earlier, Santa Claus is a translation of the Dutch word *Sinterklaas*. The story was further expanded by the 1823 poem by Clement Clarke Moore, *A Visit from St. Nicholas* (later known as *The Night Before Christmas*), in which a heavyset man and eight reindeer become established as part of the story. Santa's modern red-and-white costume is also an American invention, first portrayed in an 1863 *Harper's Weekly* illustration by American cartoonist, Thomas Nast.

Not to leave anyone out, around the globe Santa goes by many other names as well, including Kris Kringle, Grandfather Winter, Grandfather Christmas, Grandfather Frost, Christmas

Man, Yule Man, Christmas Pop, Old Man Frost, Papa Noel, Christkind, and *Babbo Natle.*

If he were alive today, my bet is that Saint Nicholas would wholeheartedly approve of my new appreciation for Santa as hero of anonymous giving. I think he'd find it refreshing and much more in line with his intent.

CREATING YOUR OWN TRADITIONS

It feels good to participate in tradition during the holidays. I wish I knew more about the generations previous to my parents, but from what I have learned as a child born in the fifties, I am the first generation in my family to celebrate with Santa. So for me the roots of the tradition are shallow at best. And despite the fact that I'm now a grandmother, it still feels to me as though my own unique Santa tradition is in its formative years. My family is always figuring it out—shopping ideas of how to do it and gathering the best ones to incorporate into our activities.

Even if the Santa who was presented to you as a child is the result of a deliberate family tradition and deep roots, you are still free to be just as deliberate in adjusting it—if for no other reason than to improve on the tradition. How could Santa mind?

Our world offers us so much information, so many options in how we do things, and where we give our attention. We are always at choice. If it all seems overwhelming to you, as it sometimes feels to me, and you sometimes wish for an established track that requires less effort and assures happier outcomes, here's an idea. Look at what makes you happier in any moment or season, focus on those aspects, and let the rest fall away. And, just like that, you have started a new tradition or steered an old one down a sweeter path.

One memory of a happy event that's worth repeating is all it takes to establish a new family tradition, like my family has. The effort in determining these new traditions is as simple as attending to what pleases you most and focusing on that. Be the bold one who begins new customs.

At my home, we start the day with Kay Kay's Fruit Loaf, symbolizing a sweet fruitful beginning. When it's time to open presents, Mark hands out assorted and sometimes odd instruments and then leads us on a parade around the house, as we joyfully make a sound that is a cacophonous mix of music and noise. After snaking through the house a couple of times, we end up back at the tree where the gift-giving begins. And there's Lynn's trail of "notes from Santa," leading from clue to clue and lastly to the largest—often the most difficult to wrap —present of the day. Starting a family tradition can make a personal mark in family history. It's your family, so why not?

The individual that you are, and the individuals that your children are, the unique way in which you interact with them, and the evolving dynamics of that relationship, are reasons enough to enjoy everything new. There is something honorable in shaping the holiday around the individuals who are sharing it, making the celebration an extension of who they are instead of requiring that they adapt to fit an old idea. If you wish, you can encourage your children to create a family tradition. The ones that are recalled excitedly the following years are the ones that have made the cut.

We needn't be stuck with the old or the literal in our celebrations. Teach only what you want to learn. **Our lives are stories and our experience of life is in how we tell those stories. Our power is in these storytelling choices.** As we shape the stories to nurture our own souls we can allow others to do the same. There might be detractors. How could there not be? Our storytelling demonstrates an exercise in freedom and a constantly evolving way of life. So our stories will always be subject to change.

The Santa story can be as simple or as elaborate as you and your children wish it to be. It can begin as one thing and morph into another. Santa is a story that can have many effects upon the listener. One thing is for sure—Santa is ours for the telling.

CHAPTER 3

THE TWO SIDES OF SANTA
CHOOSE YOUR EXPERIENCE;
SHAPE YOUR INTENTION

Ask any person on the street what Santa represents and you'll get a host of different responses. Here's some of the feedback we received:

> *My sister and I both asked for the same doll. Santa brought it for her but I was told that I had been bad and Santa only brought dolls for good girls. I was confused because I didn't remember what I had done. Then the doorbell rang and I was told to answer the*

door. When I opened the door, my doll was there and I was told that Santa had come back with it. Even though I got the doll I wanted, I remember that it was a really confusing and painful experience. In fact, when I think about it now, it's still painful.

(Lisa, age 71)

When I told my mother that the kids at school said that Santa wasn't real, her only response was, "Well, you're a big boy now." That response made me feel important and mature. I guess it was a rite of passage because I didn't feel tricked at all. I just felt good that she acknowledged me that way.

(Paul)

I was confused about Santa because my very religious grandmother told me he was evil.

(Craig)

When I was 4 or 5, my older sister told me that Santa didn't exist. I was really disappointed because I wanted to believe.

(Cara)

For many, the Santa memories are sharp and the emotions range across the gamut—joyous to painful. On one end of the spectrum, Santa represented all things good and warm and wonderful and magical; at the other end, Santa was used to punish and control and repress emotions. Now I'm not one of those crotchety old women who want to go around spoiling everyone's fun. On the contrary, I would like to see Santa celebrated in a magical way that can never be "spoiled" by honesty—in a way that can last a lifetime. That is what this book is about.

As with so many other ideas that were originally expressions of love, some people have turned Santa into a bit of a power play. As parents, there are many ways that we demonstrate our love for our children—protection, nourishment, encouragement, guidance, entertainment, and so on. And yet, we've probably all heard stories about the ways in which each of these gifts can be turned into an instrument of control.

Don't think me too harsh about our attempts to guide our children. I expect every one of us has found ourselves in a situation where bribery was the most efficient means to an end. We're not necessarily proud of it and it often comes back to bite us, but we've all likely been there. And Santa is a convenient ploy with children—used to tease and tempt them, like a prize for being good which is then turned into threat and punishment for times when they are "being bad." "*You better not pout. You better not cry. You better not shout. I'm telling you why.*" If only the song didn't have such an engaging melody!

How could it be otherwise if it is true that everything in life has its light and its dark side? The same tool that can be used to harvest can be used to commit a crime. We know love to be the sweetest of emotions and yet many atrocities have been done in the name of love. A dear friend says that every stick has two ends. We cannot pick one up a without seeing both ends, but we can choose which end gets our attention. This is true for us, and it is true for our children. Each individual chooses the objects of their attention.

Fairy tales, nursery rhymes, even lullabies have been known to frighten the very children we were seeking to entertain or amuse. When we stop and listen to the words of "Rock-a-Bye Baby," it sounds like a final farewell following a fatal fall:

> *Rock-a-bye baby, in the treetop,*
> *When the wind blows, the cradle will rock,*
> *When the bough breaks, the cradle will fall,*
> *And down will come baby, cradle and all.*

Perhaps we sing it because it was sung to us and the melody is engaging. How often are we seduced by the melodies around us but fail to hear the accompanying message? We have been hypnotized, lulled into stories that don't serve us.

Even when we are consciously presenting our best, as in giving a party with the greatest attention to detail, there is no guarantee that every guest will enjoy it. Similarly, a story told to amuse could be considered frightening to some. Santa can't be responsible for creating joy *all* of the time.

BELIEVING, KNOWING AND TRUSTING

We ask so much of our children. We want them to feel safe in the world we create for them. We want them to believe in us, know that we are doing the best we can, and trust that all will be well. And all of these concepts—believing, knowing, and trusting—are also parts of the Santa experience, so let's explore them for a moment.

"What do you believe in?" I find it interesting that in life we are rarely asked to "believe in" something other than a religion or faith. And yet we ask our children to "believe in" Santa. What are we asking? *"Believe in: To have confidence in the existence of something without proof."*[1] We want them to accept something as actual fact, without question. It is the *questioning* that becomes critical—especially since we know that the child's inquiry will eventually reveal a truth about Santa that differs from that which we earlier asked them to "believe in."

When I use the phrase "believe in," I can tell you the meaning it holds for me. If I were to say that I believe in a *concept*, then I am accepting an idea as I understand it to be—as one that works for me. If I were to say that I believe in a *Divine Source*, then I am expressing a confidence in a power and intelligence, even though it is unseen and unprovable. If I were to say that I believe in a *person*, then I would be stating my belief in that person's integrity and purity of intention. If I were to say that I believe in my *doctors*, it would mean that I expect their knowledge and skills to trump my own in determining the welfare of my body. To me, "believing in" suggests a high level of investment ranging from worship, to relinquishment of power, to simply trusting the goodness of the person/idea/thing believed in.

---

[1] www.dictionary.com

"Know" is a strong word to model for our children. We can know many things. We can know different things about the same person. We can know different experiences and interpret them and reinterpret them in order to *know* them in our memory any way we choose. We can know each other intimately or just a little. Knowing feels solid to me. When I say that I know what I want, it feels clear in my mind. When I say I know who someone is, then I have located them in my memory and placed them within a certain context that suits my own sense of identification. When I say that I know the information, I am enjoying a sense of understanding and recollection. When I say "I know what you mean," then I suspect that I have found an experience in my own life that parallels yours enough for me to appreciate your experience. When I say "I know what!" I have discovered an idea that feels right to me. Knowing is a comfortable relationship with information, people, and ideas. To me, knowing is a kind of ownership, an embracing with the mind.

"Trust" is a highly valued word for me. Trust feels solid and safe and links people in a bond. Trust is earned—and it can be broken. I have given trust to others even though it was not earned—to a roofer, for example—because I wanted a business relationship with him that was trust-worthy. However, on occasion, a disempowering situation unfolded, making me feel that the trust I freely gave was not warranted. So I came to think that trust needn't be an automatic aspect of a newly established relationship—and to think of it as a gift that I can withhold for a time without being unkind. Trust can then be given when the relationship provides a basis for it. There are levels and measures of trust. I might trust a stranger to "hold" something for me, without trusting him to "keep" it for me. However, I would certainly not encourage a child to trust someone she doesn't know as much as I sometimes do myself as an adult.

When I say that I trust an individual, I believe information that I receive from that person is truthful. This is the relationship that I most often expect and appreciate within my family and circle of close friends. Yes, trust is a word I have come to understand and use with esteem. To be trustworthy is to be honorable. Is there any better feeling than knowing that our children trust us?

The word "trust" becomes more subtle and perhaps more profound when it is applied to our relationship with ourselves. When we become more connected with our inner wisdom and more comfortable in heeding its guidance—even, on occasion, when there is no rational reason for doing so—we are employing a deep awareness of trust. Some might call this intuition and, in fact, it's really the same thing.

Studies have shown that professionals who put their lives on the line on a daily basis, such as firefighters and police, have a deep trust for their inner guidance. Most have multiple stories of situations in which a "hunch" or a "feeling" led them to a split-second decision to do the exact opposite of what would be expected in a situation and, because of that decision, they saved someone's life—or even their own.

As I have deepened my connection with this inner wisdom, my life has become exponentially more joyful. The more I align with that peaceful and joyful inner connection, the easier it becomes to trust it.

Teaching our children to tend to the little voice within that will guide them away from danger or into the most blissful of circumstances is something that can only be done by example, with encouragement that they do the same. The lessons appear in their own time; often when we are alone. Increasing our sensitivity to what "feels good" in a situation is not often emphasized in our parenting skill-set, yet doing so gives relief to any tendency to worry during times of separation and inspires confidence when the path is being laid for the first time.

When my daughter was eighteen and lived alone in the East Village of New York City, I can recall thinking about her many times late at night. Her daily work schedule required her to walk home from the subway on the other side of Manhattan in the middle of the night, after restaurants and theaters had closed and buses had stopped running. If I had not had the assurance of her strong connection to her own instincts and, importantly, the trust she had in herself, worry might have been more difficult for me to avoid. I am pleased to say that I was successful time and again in finding sleep, trusting her and the situation.

This level of trust didn't just happen; I had to practice it. Over the years, as I continue to watch my children forge their own paths, I have to consciously steer away from any seeming maternal desires for them, or attempts to control my children's choices and the resulting conditions. I recommend this course. I find it to be the sane choice for me, when other options are often painful.

Worrying about a loved one may initially feel like love in action, and it is certainly spoken of as "proof" of love. However, I have come to realize that worry is really the opposite of trust. Worry is an investment in fear. It is my goal to surround myself in relationships wherein trust abounds. In those circumstances where a relationship is too young or unproven to warrant a high degree of trust, a fearless confidence in its inevitability is what I choose to expect.

My co-author Norma remembers a sermon she heard years ago from Eric Butterworth, a well-known minister and author, that went something like this: "When people tell me that they have prayed all night long about some circumstance or other, I tell them that just because they started with 'Dear God' and ended several hours later with 'Amen,' that does not mean they were praying. They were worrying." Butterworth says that prayer is *positive* focused thought; therefore, if it's not positive, it's not prayer.

Worry is really fear of circumstances, fear of wrong choices, fear of the world in general, and lack of *trust* in any of the given elements in the story, including the person involved. Worry is a well-worn and well-demonstrated course of thought, often touted as proof of a parent's love. Taking any other mental route will most likely require a very deliberate choice, a strong intention to turn away from worry and toward the loving attitude of trust. In time this becomes the new default mode, as worry might have been before. Because I enjoy the freedom of loving without fear, I will continue to direct my thoughts away from worry, trusting my children to live the lives they choose perfectly.

Our children are invested in trusting us. As we teach them to do so, hopefully we maintain a position worthy of trust with regard to them. We are invested with their power when they are infants, and seek as their parents to transfer that power back to them as they grow into independent and confident beings. Let us empower them by using words wisely chosen and mindfully applied.

TELLING A STORY

I have heard some refer to their own childhood Santa experience as a conspiracy because adults, and principally their own parents, insisted for years that a fictitious character was indeed real. Although this is what literally happened, I think that the word *conspiracy* is a bit harsh. Surely their parents held no malicious intention in maintaining this false position for so long. Perhaps the word *scheme* or even *collusion* would fit better since the deception was constructed with such sweet intentions. These intentions, formed around words like *innocence* and *protection*, seem to have lulled us into thinking that there was no deceit involved. It's a convoluted situation.

The story we heard over and over again from adults as they recalled their Santa experience was, in most cases, almost identical. They love Santa, but they felt cheated and lied to by their parents. They were embarrassed because they had courageously defended their parents' honesty and then learned that they had been betrayed. They wanted to believe in Santa— as they would have anyway if "he" had been presented as a story—but, once they learned the truth, they were no longer able to fully enjoy the experience.

When children say they believe in Santa, it is often because they have, at some point in their experience, chosen to remain in the story, make-believing on their own. Our children's world is full of clues and evidence of the truth. There are plenty of people outside of their own home who are telling them that he is not a factual being.

I find it amusing and innocent on the part of parents everywhere that we can consider our children vastly intelligent and attentive to every other detail in life but this one? I'm beginning to think that we are better at believing in our own ability to successfully maintain the Santa pretense, than in our children's ability to discern. It is a little insulting to our kids to think that they can be so easily manipulated. If we truly think they can, then perhaps they shouldn't leave the house until they have wised up. Or until we have.

If you still don't have a quandary about presenting Santa as a person who is as real as a relative who lives in a far-away place, here's a different perspective for you. Let's flip the story around: Imagine that your young children are now teens. For years, they have come home each day hours after school ended, assuring you that they've been at a friendly happy place working on homework and extra studies. Then, over time, you hear rumors that inform you otherwise and one day you discover that they had indeed been somewhere else all along and, all the while, doing things that you don't allow.

When you confront them, they say, *"Oh, it was a game we were playing! You were so adorable when you believed the story and we just wanted to protect your innocence. You looked so happy when you were expecting us to bring you good grades and your eyes got so big with the anticipation that we just didn't want to let you down. Didn't you have fun believing in the after-school story?"*

Do you want them to tell you fairytales about sex and drugs, instead of discussing these issues with you honestly? Do you want your children to keep you innocent of the truth? After all, it is by example that we most effectively teach.

Hold on to your good intentions and come clean with yourself. This is a good time to acknowledge that when the story is told as something other than a story, Santa becomes a sugar-coated fabrication. Give your children the credit you know they deserve. They are completely capable of jumping into any story read to them or told to them AS A STORY, and still enjoying it with all the wide-eyed innocence and excitement that you could possibly generate around something you have fabricated and insisted they accept as fact. After all, they do that all the time with lots of stories, like *Shrek*, *Cinderella*, *The Little Mermaid*, *Robin Hood*, or *Finding Nemo*. Encouraging kids to blindly believe in Santa is not so different from training them to either believe anything anyone ever tells them, or to simply no longer trust us.

THE NEW SANTA STORY IS MORE, NOT LESS

Here's the rub. We thought that if we didn't present the traditional version of Santa, they would miss out on all the fun. We thought we had to make it fun for them. Yet, we can't do that. We can introduce them to what we think will be fun. But a roller-coaster that is thrilling to one will be horrifying to another. I recently viewed a video on the Internet of Santa's visit to a pre-school class. While a few children crowded around the jolly guy and accepted toys from him, a number of them were wailing and screaming in fear during his entire visit.

What we have actually been doing is making the Santa experience fun for ourselves, by creating a role for ourselves in the fantasy. All along we could have had a role in the fantasy, while keeping it a fantasy and playing with them, like any other pretending that your child already understands. When we give them a doll, do we tell them that it is a real baby and insist that they acknowledge it as such? Does their enjoyment of the doll diminish because they are aware that it is not a real baby?

Gladly, no. Baby dolls are *more* fun because they aren't real. We can switch back and forth between talking of the doll as though it were real, *"Don't you think she's hungry now?"* to referring to it as a toy, *"Did you leave your doll in the car?"* and it doesn't spoil anything. The game of playing dolls is there any time your child wants to engage in it. It never requires a faithful "believing-in" that distorts the truth.

Have you ever noticed that pretending something encourages exaggeration and delight? I know what it looks like when someone sneaks into a room. I've seen it on TV many times—sneaking around is cautiously smooth, slow and quiet, and it requires that we focus our energy so we don't attract any attention. That is the point, right?

But ask a child to show you what it looks like to sneak into a room, and they will then *pretend* they are sneaking—with exaggerated tippy-toe steps that are huge and arching, arms akimbo far out to their sides like they are walking some imaginary tightrope, and perhaps a big anxious expression on their face, or a finger held to their lips and an enormous "shhhh."

Pretending elicits loads more fun than *real*. Pretending involves choosing an emotion and wearing it like a colorful mask. A child playing an angry father will stomp into a room with hands on hips and a frown meant to frighten with its intensity. A child playing a baby will giggle and coo and be ridiculous with such delight in the play. *Playing* Santa offers much more fun than thinking there really is a Santa. Those "real" Santas can be kind of scary up close, but the ones we choose to see in our minds can always be Santas that make us happy.

Our children are not going to miss out on Santa as a fun experience if we don't insist that they believe he's real. They play make-believe all the time. The only thing we are establishing as real when we deceive is that we as parents are not trustworthy. We continue to demonstrate that, every time our children ask us about Santa and we dodge the truth.

Here's my intention: Take out the deceit and let's call Santa "a game." When one learns to "play" Santa from the start, there is no need to ever outgrow him. When you celebrate Santa with your children, you have a host of choices in the playing—many more than you might realize. Your child has more choices as well. They are no longer limited to the role of "child" in the game.

In the old paradigm of Santa, the only role for a child is one in which they ask for and expect presents. What a limited part to play. The only way for them to improve in their role is to want more and expect more. We are asking for greedy children! But let them *play* Santa in all the other ways, and we give children lots of additional channels for their amazing creative energy. They can play elf or reindeer or Santa himself. They can even play their whole life long. They can devise and construct better Santa stories and participate within the story— and the result is more than just one of greed. The result is creativity and generosity.

We make it so hard and yet it is the simplest choice of all, never requiring excuses or defense, and never resulting in the need for confession. **Let Santa be your favorite story and your favorite game—because it is such a big game and one that everyone plays.** Then start playing the game. Let's use our imaginations and talk about what Santa does to get ready for all that giving. How can Santa know what we really like, when sometimes we don't really know? Introduce the story, the game, and play it. Let your child know that whenever anyone starts talking about Santa, the game has begun. We step in and out of the game just like we do when we are playing house or playing dolls. The game is really big because so many people are playing it for so long, and it will always be a game.

This is how to enjoy Santa completely and remain completely honest in the playing.

THE SANTA PLAYGROUND

Previously it seemed that there were two choices regarding Santa: present him as real and then later be caught in the deceit, or refuse to play Santa at all. But there is a simple choice between these two extremes and it lives in the child's favorite playground, that field of imagination and fantasy.

Why did we ever opt for one of the two extremes?

- Perhaps it is because we abandoned our own sense of mystery.

- Perhaps we began to invest in the "I'll believe it when I see it" idea of life.

- Perhaps we forgot that each of us has an innate ability to create from the unseen and realize it in the seen.

- Perhaps we underestimated our child's capacity for understanding both fact and fiction and the awareness that they can exist simultaneously.

- Perhaps we lost confidence that the oak was in the acorn.

- Perhaps we felt that it was up to us to provide our child's experience.

- Perhaps we thought we could monitor another's experience simply because that person was our child.

- Perhaps we wanted to see through our child's eyes because we lost touch with the child within ourselves that never loses its innocence.

Every relationship between parent and child is different and constantly evolving. Trying to define a relationship, or process, or idea as permanent is a little like pinning a butterfly to the wall. When we do that, we still have a butterfly and it is still beautiful, but it's not the same butterfly it once was. Enjoy the organic variety and fluidity of your relationship with your child and the ideas you develop together and share in conversation and play. Playing games that constantly expand into something new is a great way of keeping ourselves malleable and expansive. Just because we are the grownup doesn't mean we are done with the growing part.

There are other points of view about Santa; some even take sides as to the validity and purpose of his presence in the holiday season. We could examine at length the ways in which the history and traditions for the holiday line up along religious and pagan paths and how commercialism might have altered their original course. Arguments might then follow along logical lines as to why anyone should or shouldn't engage in any of the strong currents of observance and participation. There are innumerable perspectives available. In my opinion, any one perspective on Santa probably has enough "facts" in the annals of history and the tenets of faith to declare it as the outstanding "winner" in a debate.

We can find something in Santa that we all like. To me it isn't that important how many generations have known him or how he might be known in another culture or country. I suspect that what matters most to you, as it does to me, is what you have known of Santa from the people in your life, and what the people in your life have known of him from you.

There are many categories within which Santa can fall: story, myth, magic, Christian, pagan, commercial, cultural, personal, pretend, traditional, sacred, sacrilegious. For me, whatever category Santa occupies could also hold Frosty the Snowman and the Easter Bunny. All three are associated with a particular season and a religious holiday, even though no religion claims them as a symbol. I like the hybrid aspect of Santa; I think it's just splendid that he can belong to the religious and the non-religious equally, to the individual and the family, to the young and the old.

Maybe it isn't that Santa himself is good or bad, naughty or nice. Perhaps the contrast is between Santa as an experience that we live for a short time with a traumatic ending or Santa as a story that we can play and enjoy in ever-expanding ways as long as we like. Perhaps if we can agree on anything during the holiday season, if we can appreciate one thing together, it could be Santa. We can even agree to each create a Santa story that works for us. And, just as each family changes its shape and dimensions each year, your family's own unique Santa story can be new each year, with fun new traditions.

Santa doesn't need more followers so I'm not proselytizing. But I don't think he needs any more naysayers, either. Like everything else in life, if you don't like the program, watch something else. Support the ones you do like. Having said that, I must also thank all of the naysayers at this juncture. It is because of the assaults on Santa, and the contrast created by those who used and abused him, that those of us who choose to love him and play with his story for a lifetime have become clearer about all of the great ways he enriches our lives. For that, I am grateful.

CHAPTER 4

THE SANTA SEGUE
FROM "BELIEVING IN" TO IMAGINATIVE PLAY

If you are about to introduce your child to the Santa story for the first time, or if you think it might be nice to re-introduce your child to Santa from a different perspective, this chapter will give you the tools for an easy segue.

INNOCENT SANTA BEGINNINGS

We all have an innate desire to love fully and deeply. As parents, this yearning takes on a special charge—we love our children unconditionally and with that love comes a desire to give to them with unconditional abandon. For many parents, the Tooth Fairy and the Easter Bunny present anonymous-giving opportunities—but there is no better opportunity to give unconditionally than playing Santa. It's our annual excuse to practice the generosity that defines anonymous giving—giving without responsive conditions; without the "thank you" part.

But to rational adults, someone must take the credit. Gifts can't just appear. If the gifts are "from Santa," the story itself needs no further explanation. Adults generally appreciate that which is *real*, not just a story. In our day-to-day lives, we are primarily focused on using our five senses to distinguish true from false, real from fake. In order to accept something that cannot be seen, we must engage in belief and faith.

Herein lies the necessity of belief, our adult ticket to accepting universal supply. Our perennial fantasy with Santa slips nearer to a religious belief when we attach to it a requirement *to believe*, a conundrum that originates in the generosity of adults en masse. By unconsciously applying adult parameters to child's play, we have confused the situation on both sides of the game.

We present Santa as real to our children and they so sweetly and innocently accept him as we describe. We are then so charmed by their childlike faith, that we dedicate ourselves to protecting that innocence, time after time striving to compile convincing argument and hard evidence. *Pay no attention to the man behind the curtain!*

For the child, on the other hand, it needn't be so convoluted. In their early years, fact, fiction and fantasy all play

My daughters at Disney World. To a child, fact,
fiction and fantasy all play out as real.

out as real. They live in an imaginal realm that not only allows them to move between real and play, but actually insists that they do. It is the way they learn so much so quickly. They question little, experience much, and assimilate what they will. It is their familiar place. Stories, toys, games—all fall within the imaginal realm of the child. Without effort, they seamlessly move between viewing a doll as simply a doll, to seeing the doll as a baby, and then back to it being simply a doll again. It is their natural process.

It is just the same for *Cinderella*—as story, as person, as story. And, unless we persist in our definition of "real," it is the same for Santa. Life is simply more magical for a child. Perhaps it is our wish as adults to become a part of that magic that makes being Santa so appealing to us every year.

The good news here is that we can still be a part of that magic:

- We can let go of making it hard and allow it be sweet and simple again.

- We can learn from our children to move in and out of the story.

- We can give them a Santa without conditional *believing in* and let them supply the fantasy that's already inherent in their playing.

- We can play Santa *with* them instead of *for* them.

When Santa is allowed to be real to a child the same way as any other story, then there is no other *reality* to maintain. In our own willingness to play, we embrace the magic with our children. We are all participants in the beautiful encompassing story that is Santa.

Santa is universally appealing to adult and child alike. Let's let go of the idea that in order to enjoy his story our children must abide by adult rules of reality. Instead let us enlist our own inner child, and embrace all things fanciful as real within our imaginations.

"BELIEVING IN" SANTA VERSUS "PLAYING" SANTA

Imagine a mother and child sitting next to each other. The mother is feeding a baby in her arms and the child is giving a bottle to her baby-doll. Both are enjoying the moment. In fact, the experience of each is more than likely enriched by the presence of the other. The parent isn't likely to point out to the child that the "baby" she is playing with isn't "real," but simply a doll.

The child is immersed in the play. She takes her own step into the imaginal realm, where the doll is, indeed, "real" during her playtime. But the child actually knows that the doll isn't real so she doesn't worry about if it is left in the car overnight or misses a feeding time, unless that is a part of her play. She steps into the imaginal realm and she steps out of it all by herself. Let's take a lesson from the way our children play. Just like playing with dolls or trucks, they can step into and out of the imaginal realm with Santa on their own.

Now, let's look at two children who are writing letters to Santa. One is lost in a rich imaginary idea of Santa that, in her childlike playfulness, seems every bit as real as the doll might have felt earlier. This child is *playing* within the story of Santa and, to an observer, there's no difference between her and her letter-writing friend sitting next to her, who *believes in* Santa as a real person and expects him to receive his letter. In fact, the little girl who *plays* Santa may have even more fun with the experience because she isn't likely to become concerned about the logistics about Santa receiving her letter. Addressing it to the North Pole and drawing a stamp on it are sufficient.

In the expanded Santa story, *believing in* Santa is eclipsed by *playing* Santa. Please understand that I'm using these labels only for your own distinction. Here's the good news: As parents, we don't need to choose between "Santa is real" and "Santa isn't real." We can simply say "Santa is a wonderful story" and then let the children do what they do best. Play. The child who *plays* Santa steps in and out of the story with the same grace that he exhibits whenever he picks up a toy.

So will the neighbor child who *believes in* be threatened by this expanded tale of Santa? The explanation of Santa as someone who lives far away—like an uncle, except that he has supernatural powers—can be easily accepted by the imaginative child, who will likely embrace the idea rather than criticize another child who promotes it. To the extent that one child's vision of Santa will prevail, it is likely that the *player* child will encourage the *believer* child to expand his vision of Santa through creative play. Sounds good, doesn't it? So, how do we get there?

(If your relative or friend voices concern about this expansion of the Santa story, I'll give you some pointers at the end of this chapter that will calm those concerns.)

THE EXPANDED SANTA STORY FOR THE VERY YOUNG CHILD

Below you'll find a story I wrote for children. The story, which I simply call *The Santa Story*, is an example of how uncomplicated it can be to play Santa with your children. If your child is very young, reading this story is a good way to introduce the expanded Santa story. I hope you enjoy reading it yourself as much as I enjoyed creating it.

The Santa Story

by Arita Trahan

Tina likes being with Mommy more than anything. Sometimes she helps Mommy and sometimes she plays with her toys. This morning, Tina is carrying an enormous stack of diapers into the nursery while Mommy puts her little brother in his crib for a nap.

Now is the beginning of their special time together. Mommy says she has something to show Tina. Tina watches as Mommy brings giant boxes in from the garage. They are going to open them and see what is inside. Mommy is excited. What can it be?

Look! It's Christmas in there! Ornaments and paper. Ribbons and a wreath. A stand for holding a Christmas tree and decorations to put around the house. With each treasure there is a story. Here is the ornament from Uncle Claude when he was in China. This is the wreath that Grandma made from the pinecones in her yard.

And there is the Santa doll that Mommy always puts on the mantle near the candles. Tina remembers the Santa doll from last Christmas and how he always smiles down at her. Tina says, "Mommy—tell me about Santa!" Mommy fluffs the white fur on Santa's coat and wipes his shiny black boots. She hands him to Tina. "Look how friendly Santa is," she says. "His story is one of my favorites."

Tina loves stories. Sometimes when Mommy reads a story Tina pretends that she is the curious monkey or the hungry bear. Sometimes she pretends that she is the friend of a powerful giant or going on a long trip in a sailing ship. Tina likes to imagine herself inside all kinds of stories.

Tina remembers a little of the Santa story and wants to hear it again. Mommy tells her that Santa is busy all year long. He finds out what children everywhere like and then plans and plans and works with all of his elves so he can give the children presents. Santa is all about giving. And Santa is always happy. Then Mommy tells Tina something new. Santa is also a game! A game that everyone can play, and play in different ways.

Tina has been learning about games. Sometimes a game has rules and sometimes it doesn't. Tina likes the made-up games best. She can play them alone or play them with friends.

Mommy says that everyone gets to be in the Santa game, even grown-ups. And there are different ways to play. Sometimes it's about elves that make presents and sometimes it's about a reindeer who shines his bright nose through a foggy night. And there are chimneys and stockings and a sack of toys and "What do you want?" and "Ho, Ho, Ho" and always,

always, always surprise gifts from Santa. Any time someone starts talking about Santa, we get to play the game.

Tina wants to play the game now. "Let's talk about the elves making all those toys!" she says. "Oh, yes!" says Mommy. "They must have some wonderful tools and be very clever to make so many different kinds of toys, don't you think?"

Just then the doorbell rings. Mommy opens the door and Mr. Lee from down the street hands a newsletter to Mommy. He looks over at Tina as she buttons the soft red coat on the Santa doll and calls out to her, "Hey, Tina, what do you want Santa to bring you this Christmas?" Tina looks at Mommy and her eyes get really big. It must be time to play the Santa game with Mr. Lee!

Tina jumps up and runs over to Mr. Lee. She pulls his arm so he leans down to hear and then she whispers loudly in his ear. "I want a really big ... DOLL!" Then she smiles at Mommy. Tina is good at this game already! She says goodbye to Mommy's friend and runs to her room to play a Santa game with her dolls.

The next day, Tina plays blocks with her friend Erik at his house. Erik says that Santa brings a Christmas tree to his family on Christmas Eve. Santa has to come in through the back door since they don't have a chimney at Erik's house. Tina thinks Erik is good at playing the Santa game too. They talk about reindeer and how Santa must land his sleigh in the backyard. Together they run to remind his dad to leave the back door unlocked for Santa on Christmas Eve!

Later, at the park Tina hears children talking about writing letters to Santa. She knows Mommy will help her with a letter. She has some questions to ask Santa and lots to tell him.

When Tina gets home, Mommy has an idea for the Santa game. She gives Tina three cards all just alike and shows her the writing on them.

Mommy reads the words "FROM SANTA," then Mommy tells Tina her idea.

Mrs. Elkins, who lives right next door, is one of Tina's favorite people. Mrs. Elkins walks very slowly and sometimes she is afraid she'll fall on the hard step in front of her house.

Mommy says that tomorrow morning Tina can go out and pick up Mrs. Elkins' newspaper where the paperboy leaves it by the sidewalk. Then Tina can put it on the mat at Mrs. Elkins' front door with one of her "FROM SANTA" cards. "Won't Mrs. Elkins be surprised?" says Mommy. "It will be our secret!"

Tina says "But I thought Santa just gave children toys." "Oh, no!" says Mommy. "Santa likes giving to everyone. Some gifts are wrapped in pretty paper and some gifts are acts of kindness. It's the secret giving that Santa shows us how to do. You'll see."

In the morning, even before breakfast, even before Tina has changed out of her pajamas, Mommy says it is time. "Quick, quick!" It is so exciting. Mommy helps Tina into her coat and hat and boots and watches at the door as Tina runs out to get the newspaper.

Tina hurries to place it by Mrs. Elkins' front door and carefully puts the "FROM SANTA" card on top. Then she runs back into Mommy's warm arms. That was fast, and she did it just right.

As Tina and Mommy eat breakfast by the window, Tina watches. And it happens. Mrs. Elkins opens her door and is about to step out when she sees the newspaper right there in front of her. She slowly leans over, picks it up, and finds the card that Tina put on top. She reads the card and then looks up the street and then down the street.

She smiles. And then she holds the card next to her heart. Mrs. Elkins is happy!

"Oh, Mommy, that was so much fun. She doesn't know it was me! And I still have two more cards. What can I do with them?" asks Tina.

Mommy walks over to give Tina a squeeze and a kiss and says, "I am sure you will think of something wonderful."

And so can you!

My story is designed to provide a wonderful Santa experience for all kids—from those just learning about Santa, to "believers" who are ready for the segue. It can also assist older children who want to teach the Santa game to their younger siblings. Once your older children are equipped with a fun story to tell to their younger siblings, worrying about them "spilling the beans" will no longer be one of your concerns. We learn best what we teach. Your children can enjoy both sides of the Santa story, the receiving and the giving, the learning and the teaching.

After reading *The Santa Story*, you may find that you've primed the pump. Lots of questions and ideas may soon tumble forth from your child.

So who gives the gifts in the expanded Santa story? Everyone, of course. Does that mean that Santa no longer comes down the chimney on Christmas Eve and leaves a pile of presents? Well, that's up to you. Any part of the old tradition can work within the context of "play." Anything you want to change is fine, too. It's your Santa *story*, after all.

THE SEGUE FOR CHILDREN WHO ALREADY "BELIEVE IN" SANTA

Even if you have already invested a few months or a few years in the construct of Santa as something "real" to be *believed in*, it's easy to transition to Santa as a story and a game. To get from where you are in the construct to where you want to be in playing the game, a conversation can move you along. And reading *The Santa Story* to a child this age is also a great way to introduce the expanded Santa story.

If your child is very young and has only recently been introduced to Santa, the segue is easy. I suggest you simply read *The Santa Story* to him and then answer any questions. You can also engage him in playing the Santa game, just as the mother does in the story. The "From Santa" cards that Tina's mother gives her are a good way to teach a child that the Santa game can be played everywhere and anywhere, and it's also a great way to introduce anonymous giving to your child.

If you have previously worked to convince your child that Santa is real and not an imaginary person, it may be tempting here to just dodge the pretense, thinking you can get away with it. If your child is very young, this might be fine. But, if you have previously addressed questions about the contradictions in the Santa construct with manufactured excuses and have concerns that your secrets will soon be revealed, then a confession is most likely called for.

Take heart in this—learning the truth now will most likely be a great deal easier on your child than learning it later. And you will both benefit in so many ways. You can restore your trustworthiness in the eyes of your child, knowing that she will be immediately consoled by getting to play the Santa game in an even bigger and better way. Your child is then less likely to "spoil" any of the fun for other children because she will have segued right into playing the Santa game as it is inspired by *The Santa Story*. If your child already knows the truth, then she has been waiting and likely hoping for this moment anyway. Keep the confession clear, brief and heartfelt, and immediately offer an invitation to play in something a lot more fun.

If your child is a bit older and you've been playing Santa for some time, it's possible that, despite all of your attempts to keep the tradition alive, the end of "believing" is already at hand. You've probably suspected that your child no longer *believes in* Santa, but tried to quell your concerns. Your experience playing Santa for your child has been fun and creative and you've felt rewarded by the whimsy of it all. However, for the sake of integrity, a confession is advised. You and your child will be better served by clearing up the pretense.

Since Santa is such a cultural phenomenon, it is a game we often enter into without an exit plan. I am reminded of the ballgames in our front yards when I was little. We didn't play for nine innings. We played until it was so dark that we could no longer see the ball. In fact, sometimes losing the ball was the signal that it was time to quit and go home. If you're like most parents, you might have some trepidation about the transition of the Santa story for your child and you want to go forward without a big upset. You'd like to be able to go home with your ball.

If you've been telling the story for a long time and maneuvering around questions and seeming contradictions, you may have concocted some elaborate schemes and squashed some budding discoveries. Thinking you are in control of the situation or at least as much of it as you are aware, you might be tempted to hold tight to the reins (pun intended) in an attempt to steer yourself clear of any blame.

For those of you who have a few years behind you, remember this—almost everyone we interviewed for this book remembers "knowing" for two years or so *before* they questioned their parents about it. That means, if you *think* it's time to cross that bridge, your kids are likely already on the other side. There are quite a few moments in their lives when you aren't around, and almost all children learn the truth from their friends.

None of us can know what is going on in the mind of another. Of course parents would like to assume that their children have told them everything that's going on with them— in their day-to-day activities and in their heads. It's amusing to me that a parent, who is fabricating a story for her child, still fully expects a fabrication-free response to all questions so she will know whether her own fabrication is still working.

Parents get so good at playing Santa that they fool themselves the longest. They don't know how to get out, so they hold on. Children find themselves in the same dilemma. They can perpetuate the idea that they still believe and stay in the "story" for several years. Some people we've interviewed indicated that even after they "knew," part of them didn't want to know, so they lived in a sort of middle-ground, believing and not believing at the same time. Children are good at balancing fantasy and fact that way. In a way they transition themselves into playing Santa safely—just as they could have all along if they hadn't been required "to believe."

> *I had two older brothers who "spoiled" Santa for me when I was very young. But some part of me kept believing anyway. It's almost like I was in two worlds—I believed and I didn't believe. I guess I just held onto Santa as long as I could, even though I had ample reason to know that it was just made-up.*
>
> *(Constance)*

Parents' attempts to keep the pretense alive often involve dodging questions by asking them back or responding with clever phrases. But that doesn't fool a child. They hear the answer in its absence. I know I did. The moment my mother hesitated in responding to my "they said he wasn't real" report, I knew that the truth was not something either of us wanted to acknowledge. I am not only referring to the truth about Santa not being real. More important at this juncture in the Santa experience is the truth about the deception and the embarrassment of having been duped.

So the question might more accurately be "How can you save face" for yourself and for your child? Children pretend they still believe for various reasons. Chief among them are: they want to make sure Santa continues to deliver; they haven't had the courage to confess; and—drum roll ... here's the most significant one—they don't want to disappoint *you.* At this juncture, most children have already put themselves in the position of protecting their parent's innocence. Can you appreciate the irony? It's especially ironic considering the number one reason parents cite for perpetuating the Santa falsehoods—*to protect the innocence of the child.* Herein the logic behind our actions has become a bit tangled.

> *Having experienced my own wounding with Santa as a child, I created elaborate Christmases for my own daughter. But when Jessica was 7, she told me that she hadn't believed in Santa for a long, long time—since she was 4 or 5—"but you were having such a good time playing it that I didn't want to wreck it for you."*
> *(Constance)*

Your child really doesn't want you to be miserable, unless she has already felt some sort of misery herself and wants you to suffer along with her. More likely she would welcome a graceful portal to openly acknowledge the truth. Your pursuit of this goal will most likely take you both to the other side without any trauma at all.

I suggest that you just go ahead and expect it to go smoothly. After all, your child has enjoyed the fantasy and, chances are, he has also survived an uncomfortable moment or two when friends told him that it was you all along. He played along on the other side of the believing game and watched you do your best to keep it going. Kids are pretty amazing at juggling fantasy and fact and blending them when it serves.

This is a natural step in the modification of the Santa fable and we should be grateful for it. We are all, parent and child, in a sort of middle-ground, aware of the deception we are all engaged in with all the various emotions attached, and seeking a way back into an honest footing with one another. Consider this a significant moment; it's a fabulous opportunity to restore the honest and candid communication channels between parent and child. Extricate yourself before the votes are in. Set an example in this moment that your children can respect and model when they are older.

Up to this point your sole desire has been to provide a blissful experience for your child. You told a tale and shaped the telling in a way that you believed would keep her happy. This is a noble goal—and yet in many ways you've set yourself up for the impossible. No one can guarantee a child's comfort or peace of mind. We can't guarantee that for anyone. We might be able to contribute toward it, but ultimately the state of a person's being is determined by that person, at every age. This is a good thing. Nurture this and encourage that, and take yourself off the hook of frustration that you can often feel trying to do everything to make your child happy. The only happy Santa experience you can ultimately be responsible for is your own.

Your relationship with your child is unique; therefore, your Santa story has played out in a unique way too. This is the beauty of parenting, isn't it? It's a learn-as-you-go proposition for each party involved.

Only in retrospect do I feel like I knew anything when my girls were young. And even today, as the mother of adult daughters, when I'm in the parenting mode I often feel that I am the one doing the most learning. The story is never over, and anything we think we have already learned continues to unfold. We are never done. This is the good news, since we sometimes feel that we have yet to get it right. *Really* right. So it is comforting to know that we are still in the game regardless of where we are in time.

If you're concerned about being a rabble-rouser or stepping on anyone's toes, this can be your personal quiet revolution. This new relationship with Santa as a story and a game can work in your relationship with your child, without undermining anyone else's relationship or anyone else's view of Santa. So if your spouse or your in-laws or your child's best friend tells a different Santa story, it's all part of the game to your child.

SANTA SEGUE SCRIPTS

The quickest, smoothest, and simplest way to segue into a new view of Santa is to assume the child already knows. Confess with the softest edges you can find. The scripts that follow are simply suggestions that will allow you to start the conversation. Once you begin, you'll find your own way to a delightful new Santa story that you and your child will both revel in.

Scripts 1 and 2 allow you to enter the conversation without first being asked:

Script 1

"I want to confess something to you. When you were little I told you that Santa was [*real / lived at the North Pole / going to bring presents to you if you were good / upset when you were naughty]* and then I didn't know how to stop treating the story as though it were real. But I like Santa being a story, because the story about Santa is so much fun and so big that it is easy for grownups and children to all play in it together. We don't have to believe that Santa is real. We can just pretend for fun."

Be honest. If you try to sneak out of it, the truth gets even more convoluted and you won't smell any sweeter.

Script 2

"I have treated you like a baby for too long. You are big enough and smart enough to know the truth about Santa and I suspect that you probably have for quite a while. I think that playing Santa *with* you can be a lot more fun than me trying to play Santa *for* you, and trying to keep you from knowing it was me. I always thought that the giving part was why Santa was so happy. I know that for me it was being Santa and giving you presents that made me happy. So maybe now you can play a part as the giving Santa too."

Scripts 3 and 4 are options when your child approaches you with a question:

Script 3

In response to, "The kids at school say that Santa isn't real.":
"Well, you know, I always wanted Santa to be real—just like I always wanted *The Velveteen Rabbit* and the other

stories that we read to be real. I thought it would be more fun for you if I convinced you he was. My imagination is almost as good as yours. So, I thought that if I played one part of the Santa story and you played the other, we could make it seem more real together. Now that I think about it, we could just as easily have played inside the story together. It would have been better if I had talked to you about this, but I didn't and I'm sorry. Now that you know the truth, we can still play together if you like. I've always had so much fun in the pretending, and this way we don't have to stop."

Script 4

In response to "Is Santa real?": "To me the *spirit* of Santa is very real. I wanted you to feel the magic that I feel, so I told you it was really Santa who brought the presents. That part wasn't honest and I don't like it anymore. I forgot that you could enjoy being a part of the magic, like I do. There really is a lot of magic happening in our lives every day, like when we [*talk about how nice it would be to have something and then "there it is" just like it was waiting for us / are singing a song and then we turn on the radio and they are playing the same song*]. I'm going to enjoy being honest with you from now on."

GROWING THE STORY WITH YOUR CHILD

After reading *The Santa Story,* begin a conversation and discuss it with your child. Simply refer to Santa using the words *story* or *game,* or discuss "playing Santa" and you are making your point. You are establishing Santa within a new and different context that emphasizes collaborative imagination and creativity. These are such wonderful tools, and your child can expand your idea of how they can be used playing the Santa game with you. This is also an ideal time to emphasize the aspects of Santa that will last a lifetime and enrich your experience of the holidays. My favorites are his boundless joy, his delight in giving, his playful use of magic, his secret way of leaving gifts, his relationship with his reindeer, his funny way of dressing, and the way he bellows his departing wish to everyone out into the quiet night. And, oh yes—his "ho ho ho!"

Here are some examples:

- "Have any of your friends ever written a letter to Santa? I like that part of the game. There are so many fun ways that children and grownups can play the Santa game."

- "Would you like to go to the mall and find a friendly-looking Santa and sit on his lap for a picture? I know Grandpa would like to have a photo of you and Santa again this year, since he likes to play the Santa game too."

- "Let's play the Santa game. What do you imagine Santa is doing right now?"

- Find another book or a movie about Santa and discuss it. "Oh, look, this story about Santa is my favorite." If it's a book and there's a picture of the author on the back or the book-flap, point to the photo and say, "Here is a picture of the person who thought of this story about Santa."

- "Those magical reindeer are amazing. How do you think they might get ready for that long night pulling the sleigh through the sky? Do you think they feel good working with their friends to make so many people happy?"

- Compare Santa with other stories: "The elves that help Santa remind me of the munchkins in *The Wizard of Oz*. They are so much fun to watch. Why do you think they are having so much fun?"

- "Why do you think the story says that Santa lives at the North Pole? Wouldn't it be funny if he lived on a tropical island? How would the story be different then?"

- "I was thinking about how our friends enjoy the Santa story and wondering what I would like Santa to take to them. What kind of present do you think would be the best surprise for your friends, _____ and _____? Perhaps we could play Santa for them!"

- "When I think of Santa, I think of giving all kinds of gifts. I know that sometimes there are gifts that can't be wrapped and put under a tree. Can you think of gifts like that too?" With this one, you are putting an emphasis on acts of kindness.

- "Remember that time you gave a gift to _____ and [*he/she*] was so happy. Why do you think it made [*him/* her] so happy? Did it make you happy too?"

- "I like that Santa is so jolly. Do you know anybody like Santa? Someone who is always giving presents? What else do you like about Santa in the story? Do you ever laugh like Santa?"

- "If you could climb inside the Santa story, would you like to visit Santa and help him with his work? What would you like to be in charge of doing? Maybe there's something we could do together."

Engaging in the fantasy together and playing all sides of the story allows children to expand their appreciation of the Santa experience and to embrace more possibilities for it in their own lives. There are limits to playing only one role, a role that required that they decide what they wanted to get from Santa and then waiting for him to deliver the goods. But now, playing the Santa game opens up all kinds of possibilities. By using their imaginations, they can play it for a lifetime.

When you have crossed the bridge from pretense into the Santa story as a game, you will find that the fantasy is

as strong—and likely even stronger—because its integrity cannot be compromised. You have cemented a new view of Santa that is as real as the previous one but this new, improved Santa is no longer at risk due to rumors that he is fictional.

We begin to practice a new approach to stories and storytelling. We can selectively integrate all that we want—and only what we want—into our lives. We are in charge of our own stories with the simple goal that what feels good for the individual is what makes that story a good one for them. We are practicing integrity and still enjoying the fantasy.

When we make such bliss our goal and teach that to our children, then we transcend innocence and naiveté. We learn to create a fulfilling life-story that belongs to us so completely that it cannot be diminished by anyone else, regardless of the stories they tell.

HOW CAN A NON-PARENT RESPOND TO THE "SANTA QUESTION"?

Tip-toeing around the Santa question can be challenging for relatives and friends. Does the child still "believe"—or not? Most people will go to great lengths to avoid any possible conflict, considering the Santa relationship to be a personal issue between parent and child.

So what if a beloved child in your life comes to you in confidence and asks the burning question: "Is Santa real?" Just remember, this moment didn't come out of thin air. Any child who asks this question has likely deliberated for some time and come to conclusions of his own.

When a child approaches you, the non-parent, with this question, it indicates that he has a high degree of trust in you as an adult. He expects that you are going to be straight with him. How do you meet that child's expectation while continuing to honor the relationship that you have with his parents?

A wise and cautious response is one that first puts the ball back in the child's court: "What do *you* think?" or "Why are you asking?" or "What do you think I'm going to say?" Convey this responsive query in a way that the child will interpret as sincere and interested, rather than in any way flip. Assure the child that he has your full attention with encouraging eye contact.

If the child says, "I think my Mom and Dad are Santa," he has taken the essential first step on his own. You can now go ahead and acknowledge that this is true. If he says, "I think my Mom and Dad are lying to me," you can soothe the situation. Either way, you now have the perfect opportunity to explain how much fun his parents must have had in playing Santa for him. You can admire their secret generosity as acts of anonymous giving—and also as ongoing evidence of their unconditional love for him.

You get to be the special adult who welcomes him into a wiser, honest acceptance of what is true, while also helping him to appreciate his parents from a wider perspective. At this juncture in his young life, you are guiding him through a rite of passage, welcoming him into "big kid" status. And now you can invite him to *play* Santa too. Perhaps you'll want to read *The*

91

Santa Story that's found earlier in this chapter and then discuss how he can play Santa for someone else—or how the two of you can join forces to play Santa together.

To recap, here are the four steps:

1. Acknowledge the truth
2. Welcome the child into the more mature status of "knowing the whole story"
3. Invite the child to play Santa
4. Encourage the child to proudly tell his parents about his discovery and his new intention to play Santa as well

Any likelihood that the child will find fault with his parents for previous deceptions is diminished when he is both validated for his cleverness and acknowledged as worthy of playing Santa himself. This conversation between you and the child will likely serve his parents in ways they may never know.

If you do not encourage the child through the fourth step of talking to his parents, it is very possible that he might continue to keep his revelation from them. Children have their reasons for delaying this step in the process. If they are not ready, you might want to make it clear that you are not inclined to deceive anyone, and that if the parents ask you what you know, you will be honest with them too. The years of "getting your stories straight" in order to maintain the believing could be coming to a welcomed end.

Most importantly, do what feels right and honorable to you in the situation. Know that you are setting an example for this child in the way he perceives his parents and in the way he celebrates the Santa story from this point on in his life.

You are at a critical juncture, and it is yours as well as the child's. This is your rite of passage from the adult who "plays along" to the adult who "leads into clarity and kindness."

SHARING THE NEW SANTA STORY WITH RELATIVES AND FRIENDS

Like most new ideas, when you share "Santa as a game" with other adults some will cheer you on, while others may feel that you're trying to knock an icon off his pedestal and suggest that it's simply easier to deal with the status quo Santa.

Here's a summary of ways Santa is enhanced by playing the Santa game that may be helpful:

- **Focus on anonymous giving**
  The emphasis in the new Santa story is on teaching anonymous giving, both in the form of gifts and acts of kindness. The child has an active role in this story and uses her imagination to come up with new ways to *play* Santa and *be* Santa.

- **Every child can create and believe their own version of the Santa story**
  The new expanded Santa story doesn't impinge on anyone else's version of Santa. Children who learn to

play the Santa game can easily play alongside other children who still *believe in* Santa, without putting anyone's belief at risk. Children who *play* the Santa game are so engaged in it that they accept any other child's way of playing Santa.

The child who is playing within the Santa game doesn't have any rules to follow. He easily steps in and out of the story with the same grace that he exhibits whenever he picks up a toy. He doesn't have to "believe" this or that.

It's an embracing, all-encompassing type of game. In short, a child who is *playing* Santa within the Santa game simply won't feel the need to challenge anyone else's Santa story.

- **With the "Santa game" everyone gets to play and is, in fact, already playing**

  The parent introduces Santa as a game that is already being played by practically everybody else. Any child's version of the Santa story is embraced within the context of play by the child who is enjoying the Santa story *as a story*. The moment that anyone starts talking about Santa the game has begun.

- **A child's Santa story can incorporate any family traditions**

  Let's say that every year Santa brings the tree to your house on Christmas Eve. The fact that Santa brings the tree to a friend's house three weeks earlier doesn't mean there is an inherent contradiction in Santa. It just means other people are playing the game differently. Santa can come down the chimney or through the front door. Anybody can play any way they want.

- **Multiple Santas can make the Santa game even more fun**

  It's okay if multiple Santas show up within the same city block because all of those Santas are *playing* the Santa game. Instead of a child questioning which one of the Santas is real or being told that one of them is simply "Santa's helper," in the world of *play,* Santa can show up frequently and in quantity. How fun that we have lots of Santas! That's even more joy.

- **With the Santa game, a child has numerous mentors in anonymous giving**

  Along with enjoying the gifts received from an anonymous giver, children can simultaneously appreciate how parents—both their own and others—along with other adults in their lives, are busy playing the role of Santa. They are now able to see their parents as mentors in the joyous realm of generosity. Receiving from anonymous givers makes our entire world feel abundant and kind. Without the obligatory "thank you," it is often easier to feel genuine appreciation. When we, as children or adults, become aware of the multitude of Santas giving with such joy, it creates within us a sweeter worldview. A verse in my song *I'm Being Santa* explains this nicely:

> *Look around—the world is full*
> *Of happy, sweet surprise,*
> *And everywhere you turn, you'll see*
> *There are Santas in disguise.*

When we are *playing* Santa, gratitude grows, greed diminishes, and giving becomes even more fun.

You can hear the song, *I'm Being Santa*, on my website, *www.TheSantaStory.com*. The music video of the song is also on the website, as well as the opportunity to submit your own video performance of the song.

CHAPTER 5

SANTA AS CATALYST
WHAT PLAYING SANTA REVEALS TO US ABOUT OURSELVES

Like so many of the important stories in our lives, the Santa story and how we relate to it gives us an opportunity for choice and contrast. There is so much on our menu to choose from at this time of year, it can sometimes take a while to sort it all out. In the process, it seems that Santa and his season elicit from us more than we might have ever known we possessed in opinions, priorities, and emotional responses.

SEASONS OF EXPERIENCE

The Santa season is filled with extreme experiences. It is a time of great creativity expressed in music and entertainment. Some of our most enduring melodies and movies were produced for this season and are enjoyed perennially during it. It is a time of emphasis on family, gathering together, exchanging gifts, and acknowledging our heritage and traditions. It can be a time of extreme activity, a time when the individual can feel that much is required of him by family, friends, religion, and community. For some, doing the holiday "right" requires days of baking and elaborate displays both indoors and outdoors. It can be a time of reflection as well as celebration. We sometimes find unexpected emotions welling up as we think of these expectations or focus on a loved one who is no longer with us or now lives at a distance.

This is the one time each year when many adults allow themselves to fully participate in the fantasy-world that children enjoy all year long. Some tap into extreme measures of make-believe with the perfect excuse that they are doing it for their children. Some, trapped on the merry-go-round of "I've got to make it better every year," believe that they must play a flawless Santa to assure that their children continue to come along for the ride. Their desires to make the holiday perfect may not simply be for their children's benefit but may also extend from their own past Christmases. Some wish to re-live delightful memories of magic, while others still strive for the magic that they did not have themselves as children.

The Santa season seduces with its promise to surprise and gift us—filled with Hallmark images of peace and love. Sometimes we expect so much, from ourselves and others, that we are emotionally and physically spent when the circumstances of our lives undermine our intentions. The heightened energy at this critical time of year sometimes reveals more about us than there seems room or time to deal with amidst all the activity.

Even after they no longer believed in Santa, one friend related that her mother, who was a widow, was always determined to give each of her two daughters Christmas gifts of equal value. But since the gifts themselves never cost exactly the same amount, every year she would give one of the girls an envelope with cash to made up the difference to the penny. What an effort that woman went to in her attempt to show each daughter that they were equally loved. How much of an emotional toll did that take?

As I listened to the stories we gathered in writing this book, I realized that Santa and the season he represents serve as a catalyst, exposing who we are at our core—throwing us into the stream of life where we bump into each other and express ourselves and discover more and bump into each other again. There are as many different ways to play Santa as there are people playing. And each season of their playing evolves into something new yet again. Tradition doesn't stop each moment from expressing as no moment has ever expressed before.

Whenever I find myself feeling set in my ways about how I play Santa, it benefits me to listen to another's story. I often hear new perspectives that I find expansive and that reawaken me to the variety that life offers. As each person continually makes and shapes her own experiences, a multitude of *right* choices and responses unfold. Sometimes the choices and responses that have brought us to harmony now had their roots in discord.

Lynn told me about her granddaughter who proclaimed repeatedly that she hated Santa and everything about him. Why? Because she never got what she wanted. Yes, she got stuff, but never what she *wanted*. Lynn explained that this particular granddaughter always asked Santa for gifts that were not plausible for her family at the time. To me it seemed that Lynn's granddaughter had used her wish list as license to dream big. She then took the opportunity to disapprove of anything less than the full extent of her dreams manifesting in her life.

I can appreciate both the expansive and the disagreeable in this Santa story. It's great to dream big and, at the same time, from the grandmother's point of view, it may not be fun to play with people who expect more than we are willing or able to offer. Lynn and her granddaughter both seemed to be expressing themselves honestly to each other, each being true to themselves in the story. Perhaps there was some small degree of stubbornness in their shared Santa experience that each of them mirrored back to the other. Ah ... families and Santa.

Lynn also told me of an instance when she had played Santa years before with one of her daughters who "was always, always a problem." This daughter also knew what she wanted and would sometimes take it at the expense of others. Their family tradition was that the presents that Santa put in the stockings were wrapped with tissue paper instead of the heavier wrapping paper used for the Santa presents under the tree. The year that this child was in kindergarten, she got up on Christmas Day well before anyone else was awake and proceeded to unwrap everything in all of the stockings, decide what she wanted in hers, and then redistribute all of the items. The little girl reassigned to her own stocking all the cosmetics that had been put in her aunt's stocking.

The next morning it was apparent to everyone that something was amiss. In addition to the odd distribution of gifts, all of the stocking presents were minus their tissue wrapping. Since Lynn had to maintain that the stockings were all *Santa's* doing to protect the Santa construct she had created, she couldn't say anything. Later she found the missing tissue-paper wrapping in the outside trash can, evidence of her daughter's tampering, and confronted her. Lynn eventually extracted a confession but one without remorse. Her daughter was very proud of what she had done.

So the following year, Santa left presents as usual for everyone under the tree, but in her stocking this child got coal and sticks wrapped up in tissue paper along with a few small toys. Lynn had wanted to make the point that Santa knew she'd been naughty. Lynn was dismayed that it made no apparent difference to the child or her future behavior. She told me that she had recently talked about all this to her now-adult daughter, who still considered that visit from Santa in which she re-gifted the stockings one of the most fun times she ever had.

Incidentally, Lynn reported each of these Santa experiences to me with great gusto and pride. I could imagine her as the sort of mother and grandmother who would, in her own way, encourage and delight in a strong and occasionally rebellious spirit. As I listened, I was surprised to find myself rather pleased with the coal and sticks part. I would never have thought of myself as one to embrace the dark side of Santa this way. I am glad I have not been appointed the job of judging the choices someone else has made—either mother or child. But if I were, I think that they all did very well within the experience they created together.

The night before the interview with Lynn, I had been at Target. While standing in line to check out, I became intrigued by a beautiful little boy. He was busy looking at the variety of candies at the display near the registers while his mother checked out. He must have been around four and I was entranced.

I heard his mother call to him as she finished her transaction and pushed the cart along with an equally beautiful girl-child in the infant seat. What a lucky mom—such wonderful children! She urged him to join her so they could leave. He popped out to show her a big candy bar and asked if he could have it. She replied that she had already paid and it was time to go. He said, "Go on, and I'll catch up!" to which she continued her urging. He repeated himself several times but was now hiding behind the display in such a way that he was no longer visible to his mother.

I could see him and I could see that he was trying as hard as he could to push that huge candy bar into his pants pocket ... and he was succeeding. Did the pocket extend to his knee? Apparently. I was now horrified. His mom was wending her way with the cart back to find him, but she was not there in time to see what he had done. Just at that moment, another register opened up and the cashier called to me to accept her assistance. As I walked toward her I passed the mom and leaned in to tell her about the candy bar. I heard her say, "Put that back. You can't take something like that without paying for it," and his reply, "Then pay for it, because I want it." It was important to me that the Target mother not reward that child's behavior by buying that candy bar. In the end, though, I don't know what she did, as I moved on to the checkout.

I also knew that at least two cashiers had been aware of the little boy's pilfering, without any apparent plans to do anything. Was I the only one who cared? It puzzled me. I think I was most disturbed that he had so charmed me with his innocent good looks prior to his theft. Do I expect or require more of some than of others? What makes one look innocent to me and another not?

This experience compounded my unrest the following day when I first heard the story about the young girl's stocking ruse. Together these stories provided a disturbing insight into my own sense of justice and goodness. I discovered that I might be less likely to defend an adorable and innocent looking youth than I might an older and experienced one. And I might be more easily outraged when what looks innocent is not.

Perhaps I have an unconscious belief that we each have our expected roles to play, and I'd rather feel that I have at least cast each character correctly in terms of my expectations. Regardless, I am glad that my vote on the situation is not required, for my surprising vindictiveness is not something that pleases me. How glad I am that the Santa in my story gives unconditionally. If he were less wonderful he might reward some and punish others, as I seem prone to do in the heat of the moment. I love Santa, who is full of overriding generosity and joy. I like having his example to follow.

SEASONS OF CHANGE

Santa and the Santa season can feel vastly complicated for us on so many levels. There were times in my younger adult life when my Santa story matched my life with more grace and ease than at other times.

You see, Santa and I have had our rough moments. We have broken up and made up several times. However, I believe the whole process has improved our relationship vastly. That is because it was in the awkward moments that I discovered the most about myself. It was when things weren't so wonderful that I identified some unsuccessful holiday patterns in myself that I no longer wished to perpetuate.

Like traditional family meals, sticking with the old menu during the holidays may make for easier planning, but doesn't necessarily satisfy the current appetites of the family gathered. We keep changing, and some of the old recipes just don't taste as good as we seem to recall. Sometimes it is hard to remember who liked something in the first place, when no one seems to like it now.

We are not the same group that we once were. There are new members and missing members and vegetarians amongst us now. How can we keep tradition and be flexible at the same time? There's so much to do. Is there time to change in the middle and still feel good? And therein lies the qualifier. We all want to "feel good" about who we are, what we do, and how it all fits together. We want a Santa relationship that works. There were, for me, many personal choices that never ended up feeling good. Eventually, I chose to choose again.

The Santa my parents introduced me to was really only suitable for the very young. During my teen years I continued to appreciate the gifts I received but found the most pleasure gazing up through the lights of the tree and listening to favorite music. Those Christmases were somewhat melancholy for me. Our immediate family was so small and the festivities that involved me did not extend beyond our own small circle. My brother was also past the "Santa years" so there was no longer a child to make a show for. It all felt shallow and disappointing on a deep level. My mother often expressed her dismay that I was "growing up so fast"—she seemed to yearn for the younger Arita and the fun we had *then*. I suppose I did, too.

When I married, I found myself in a much larger family circle with several adult children and their mates. The traditions of this family, inspired by their rich German heritage, extended to all kinds of special delicacies and delights. The best news was that it was all new for me and, as a new member of the family, I felt especially welcomed. There was special holiday bread and each person had their own personalized hand-knit stocking. I got mine right away on that first Christmas of my marriage. It was large enough to hold a treasure trove of well-thought-out treats for a "child" of any age. Filled to the brim, these stockings were placed at our assigned seats at the large dining table on Christmas morning. Once everyone had gathered, the first step of eating breakfast and opening all the gifts in the stockings could easily last an hour or more. In addition to the personal items and toiletries that yielded from the stockings, there were often small games, a contest or two to figure out, and perhaps a shape puzzle or a tiny jigsaw puzzle to assemble. These games and contests were a special joy to me, and I often felt that the prizes given to the contest-winner were selected with me in mind.

Breakfast and stockings were a relaxed and unhurried event, as people wandered into the dining room in their pajamas. Even the pajamas were part of the festivities as each of us was given a new pair; it was the one present we had been allowed to open from Santa the night before.

Finally, leaving our piles of "stocking gifts" at our places at the table, we took time to dress. Then we reassembled and moved to the living room and the piles of presents that were waiting beneath the tree. Santa's elf—the youngest among us who was capable of the task—then began the process of picking up a package, discovering the recipient of it, and delivering it to that person. This adventure in identifying all of the relatives who had come from near and far was sometimes a little daunting to a youngster, but by the end of the job, the names of all of the assembled aunts and uncles and cousins had become familiar.

One-by-one, the presents were stacked beside each of us, always the same number of items in each pile. Then the opening began. One at a time, the wrapping was admired, scissors passed, trash collected, and the reveal of the gift appropriately "oohed" and "ahhhed." Gratitude was expressed, gifts passed around for all to see, and sometimes a fashion-show ensued. Santa was always my in-laws. All other gifts had tags, labeling the gift-givers as other members of the family. There was no hurry. It was a celebration I thoroughly enjoyed.

I don't recall a specific menu that was served at my in-laws' home every year, but each meal was wonderful and special. Lots of cookies were made for eating, with dozens more given on large platters to neighbors and friends. If it sounds as though this family really appreciated Christmas and did a magnificent job of it, you're right. My mother-in-law's family loved the holiday so much that they even founded a theme park in Santa Claus, Indiana, which is now called Holiday World. A treat for all ages, in those early years it was a simple park that housed mechanical toys, miniature trains, gingerbread houses, nutcracker soldiers, and dolls—all collections from their German ancestry. Later it became a theme park on a grand scale.

Some years later, as a newly single-again mom, I grabbed my kids and took them to my parents' house for Christmas. My brother and his family had already begun their own tradition of spending the night there, even though they lived close by. I liked being all crowded together. It was a good beginning in preparing for Santa's visit. But the next morning erupted like an energy storm.

Along with my children, I stood and watched as their two cousins rushed to open everything at once. There were squeals of excitement and chaos, paper and toys knee-deep everywhere.

I remember my younger daughter, having been taken by surprise, turning to me at some point near the end and asking, "Did they open the presents from us yet?" None of us could tell. When the dust settled, my girls and I found our way through the morning. Then we sat down to the exact same meal that my parents prepared for Thanksgiving. It was a tradition.

As much as this sequence of events at my parents' house seemed to work for everyone else, it wasn't really a match for me. And now I also had to deal with alternating Christmases, sharing the girls with their dad. I disliked the idea of taking turns; I didn't want to deal with competing Santas.

So I reviewed the situation. If I relinquished celebrating Santa at my house there would be consolation prizes for me. I wouldn't have to get everyone to agree on what we were going to do together as a new, smaller family, or overwhelm them with my own choices. I wouldn't have to continue the traditions of my in-laws or my own family, neither of which seemed appropriate at the time. I would be free to dismiss the obligatory nature of the holiday that required attendance and compliance. There would be no struggle with their dad over which part of the day we each got. I could enjoy my children on some other day in a more relaxed environment that was easier to shape into whatever pleased us at the time.

That became my choice. From then on, I always sent my kids to their dad's for Santa. In later years when they celebrated the holiday with me as adults, I was assured that my daughters were with me as a matter of choice and not out of obligation. The anxiety of the season could belong to everyone else. We celebrated a post-holiday gathering and less structured gift-sharing in a thank-goodness-that's-over kind of way.

But where was the tradition? There is something very soothing in a tradition. It's like an old robe, pulled out of the closet all warm and worn and sunk into without having to think about it much. Santa wasn't mine anymore. Could I replace Santa?

I thought of creating a new tradition suitable to what I felt we had become as a family—my children, my new husband, and me. Gathering information about the winter solstice, I came up with ideas for celebrating the longest night of the year, which falls between December 20 and December 23 in the northern hemisphere. (For those who live in the southern hemisphere, the winter solstice falls between June 20 and June 23.)

I learned that the winter solstice is celebrated for an entire day but it actually occurs as a split second in time when, due to the tilt of the earth, the hemisphere leans farthest away from the sun and therefore daylight is shorter—and the night longer—than any other day of the year.

For my new solstice ritual, I chose to place special emphasis on the sun and how much we had missed it during the days with less hours of daylight that had preceded this—the shortest day of all. We would celebrate how glad we were that longer days were returning to us. I thought that going without electricity during the evening hours would be an adventurous start. During this shortest day of sunlight, we would "harvest" fire from the sun, and then use that fire to light the longest night, taking its promise with us into that darkness.

I used a magnifying glass to start a small fire during the brightest moments of the short day and lit a special solstice candle. This harvest from the sun was the only fire we used—spreading it around the house by lighting other candles, as well as the fireplace that served as our source for both food and warmth. I even bought special cast-iron cookware for cooking over the fire, and planned a meal accordingly.

We entertained ourselves with games and music and conversation late into the night and marveled at how long and dark the night was. In the morning we welcomed back the sun with a celebratory breakfast and exchanged gifts.

The solstice celebration was a great slumber party but it didn't make it as a new tradition. The first year, in order to catch the bright mid-day sun, I had to start the fire with the magnifying glass before my daughters arrived. That was a disappointment because I thought it would be fun to do it together.

On the following years, our plans were waylaid when they were unable to travel in time for the solstice altogether, due to their college schedules. My attempt at creating a new family tradition had been fun, but the winter solstice just didn't have the cultural support to give weight to it as an important holiday. I also realized that I was trying to do more than just reinstate the solstice holiday. I held myself responsible for the undoing of old traditions and assigned myself the job of filling the void. I wanted to manufacture an experience for all that would surpass ... Santa.

But I missed Santa.

SEASONS OF IMPROVISATION

I lived in Santa limbo for a few years. My new husband, who had never celebrated with Santa, offered no input; nor did he see a necessity for celebration of any sort. He was, however, happy to play along in whatever way I preferred. So, I got selfish (in the sweetest sense of the word) and began to consider which of the various elements of Santas past I liked the most. I thought of all that Santa inspired—the giving and the togetherness around the gifts. Surely I could begin again with the Santa story, keeping it simple and making certain it remained true to my present self.

One way I played Santa was by giving my children most of the ornaments they treasured in their youth for their own Christmas trees. I have enjoyed watching as they have created their own traditions. They make special cookies and gingerbread houses. They devise extremely creative cards to send to friends and family. Their mates add their own ideas and I am looking forward to watching how they play Santa with their children. I would like to think that we each do only what we love best, nothing else and nothing less.

I am relieved to report that one less-than-happy aspect of the holiday that underpinned my entire experience for years and years has now fallen by the wayside. I suspect you might recognize this aspect in your own life. It began in my years as a teen and flourished during my early years as a mother. It appeared like clockwork, warping the entire season. It was *expectation.* As much as I delight now in flexibility and improvisation, I must admit that these are acquired and cultivated skills. The truth is that I was born a control freak. Give me a season, or a gathering, or an excuse, and I can drown in the minutia of details, taking down everyone within my reach. If I were a young mother these days Martha Stewart would have to move over!

I remember early preparations for the family holiday gathering when my children were little ones. I taught them poems and songs and scripture to recite at self-appointed moments. I rehearsed readings of special articles and stories that I personally performed for the family. And I always imagined the responses to these performances: The family would be moved to laughter and tears. We would cherish each other and the time together and the gifts of verse and narrative.

Well, so much for my expectations! What usually happened was something else altogether. First of all, in order to assure an audience for these important performances, I would have to convince everyone in my family that life would go on if the television was turned off for a short time. Then, at the designated time, when all eyes turned their way, my children would grow suddenly shy. (Later, during their baths, with me as their sole audience, they would once again be ready and eager to perform.) My own solo performances did not fare much better. Just as I would reach the climax of the story-reading, my mom would get up and go to the kitchen for some more coffee.

It felt as though there was a conspiracy underway. How dare they insist on diminishing my efforts to enrich the season with all my creativity and passion? How dare they prefer to relax in front of the TV with a cup of coffee when, clearly, it was the time for more important, more memorable, more "seasonal" activities? As you can surmise, I spent a great deal of every family gathering in a self-imposed state of disappointed victimhood.

Thank goodness for my children. They are so resilient, so flexible, so creative, and so willing to use the moment to improvise their own enjoyment. I eventually learned from them. Perhaps the bathtub was the best time for those recitations after all. My mother always said that I was born "a little old lady." Surely she was referring to my serious nature. Well, if I saw my life through a sober lens in my youth, I give myself permission in my mature years to be more childlike and easy, and at least to imagine myself as a very playful adult. Today I choose care-free over care-ful.

My long lists of plans before a gathering have not diminished. Are you kidding? They have multiplied. But not to worry—I am no longer insisting on a "better season done *my* way." Instead, I am offering a varied menu of ideas, timetables, recipes, and activities. I appreciate that my children are inclined to do the same. They bring with them their own lists of ideas for fun, games, puzzles, requests, and willingness to play— whether together or separately. I like to think that we are each bringing our best to our family table—and we can only do that when we take care of ourselves first and fully.

This also means being honest about where we feel flexible and where we don't. In most cases, I find that flexibility increases when we know that we can respect each other's inflexibility as well. I now give myself permission to not participate if I don't want to—a radical type of freedom—and this generally allows the idea of participation to appear more attractive. Freedom is our base. Joy is our goal. Expansion and growth are the result. We get better and better at who we are as individuals and how we relate as a family.

This year I feel as though I am embracing Santa anew. My dad, following my mother's recent passing, gave me the big, flocked artificial tree they had enjoyed for years. I am eager to design its decoration this year as my special treat to me. My husband will likely participate in the eggnog and the gifting and being with friends, and anything else that inspires him. He always eagerly acknowledges how beautiful I make things. I would guess that the music, the entertaining, and being with friends are his favorite aspects of the season. In our unique, individual ways, each of us will enjoy the event and remember and celebrate what is important to us. Santa is my favorite symbol. And each time I climb into the Santa story, I make it my own.

I am not a "special day" kind of gal. I would rather NOT receive roses on Valentine's Day from my husband. If he wants to bring me flowers, which I love, I prefer them on any other day. They mean more to me then. It's my style. We share our own symbols of our romance. Silly made-up-in-the-moment songs that he sings to me. Inside jokes that grew out of difficulties we survived. The baby-talk we use with our pets. Getting sentimental over the same things.

These are our romantic expressions. They are not seasonal. When we find ourselves at a card display prior to Valentine's or any other social holiday, we pour over them and show favorites to each other. We enjoy the sweetness of the sentimental ones and relish the ones that make us laugh. We rarely opt to actually purchase the cards unless we see one that makes us think of someone else and decide to buy it for them. For Valentine's Day, this card-display sharing is often all that we do in a commercial way. It's *our* tradition. And we love it that way.

When it comes to the Santa season, I love most that nothing is required of me. I am free to do and be as pleases me the most. And while I am doing and being that, the effect for my family is freedom for them to be and do what pleases them the most. When we gather, it is perfect. When we do our separate thing, it is perfect. There is opportunity in each Santa season to explore who we are and what we choose and then enjoy it. I delight in watching how my children express themselves in their choices. Even when their choices may appear to be like someone else's, I celebrate the awareness that their motivation or interpretation is always their own. How perfect for me that when it comes to Santa's day it doesn't matter to me if my children are in another state. I support them in being where they are the happiest. And any day that we are together is a holy-day.

We have evolved to this new worldview, and will evolve into more. There was more structure when they, and I, were younger. It suited us then. What suits you? What have you grown past? Ask yourself often, and lean in the direction of more joy, more peace—or at least in the direction of whatever will afford greater relief. Your state of joy will color the world around you and it will be appreciated by all. This is not to say there they might not be some who expect you to play into their game and even assume a particular role. And you can, if you wish, imagine a way to do this and still be true to yourself. Ultimately, it is you being happy that will contribute the most to any circumstance.

SEASONS OF IMAGINATION

Every parent who approaches Santa was also once a child who had some sort of experience with (or without) Santa. We have laid that foundation and choose how we build on it. And since so much of life is cyclical, we get to choose over and over and over as the years go by. Just because we keep choosing differently doesn't mean that we have ever chosen wrong. It might just mean that we are interested in the effect or experience that a different choice might offer. There may not be any going back, but there is always a going on.

Lynn kept moving on. The same woman with the granddaughter who hated Santa, and the daughter who created the stocking fiasco continued to play Santa her own way, regardless of the personal response of each individual with whom she played. Recently she was hosting the Santa experience for a grandson. He had enjoyed opening all of his Santa presents and then saw a card pinned to the tree with his name on it. In the card Santa had written that one of his gifts was too large to put under the tree, and he should go look in the den near the TV. There he found another card that led him to another place, and then another, with the final note saying, "Oh, it fits under the tree after all!" At this point her grandson ran to find his new bicycle parked next to the tree. His response was, "Was it here all along? But I couldn't see it before!" The treasure hunt had inspired him beyond surprise, into a place where the visible can become invisible and back again. Lynn had been simply looking for a fun way to reveal the bike without having to wrap it. The child saw it as an exercise in magic.

The cast of characters that surround your Santa story is going to be unique. Make it your own. Catch yourself so you aren't swept into what feels like someone else's idea. Use Santa, enjoy Santa, pass him around and see what he elicits from you and others in your life. Play with Santa and watch the game evolve. Keep the Santa idea malleable and it will fit more easily and gracefully into your life as he engages with one generation after another.

If I were you, what would I do? Why—exactly what you are doing. Only you can receive the inspiration that is going to perfectly match your heart and your circumstances. As I write this book, I could be concerned that what I think at the end might not match what I thought at the beginning. Here's trusting that none of it is so dogmatic that it doesn't allow for flexibility throughout. If I were to go back and make changes for how I am constantly looking at things anew, then I would never stop and publish. Evolution gallops on.

We are playing with mythical figures and cultural archetypes here. The playing field is huge. Play small or play big. Play it safe or play with reckless abandon. Have fun. Let Santa inspire you.

CHAPTER 6

THE GHOSTS OF SANTAS PAST
REVISITING SANTA IN YOUR LIFE STORY

Despite the joy that Santa brings to most children, as we interviewed people for this book, my coauthor Norma and I also heard reports of parents who used Santa to threaten and punish. We heard histories of those who felt left out because their families didn't celebrate Santa or maligned him for a variety of reasons. The effect was a chorus of conflicting, often bittersweet Santa memories. Some more bitter; some more sweet.

For those who have less than delightful memories regarding Santa, it's not too late to heal those memories. I started writing this book simply to share the Santa story that had come to me spontaneously when my older daughter first asked about him at the age of three, wanting to offer the "story" that worked so well for me as an alternative for other parents. As my tale unfolded within the context of these memoirs, the very telling of it and revisiting of those past events led to a much welcomed personal healing. I found myself in a process that proved to be liberating.

MY SANTA GHOST STORY

My own Santa memories as a youth were not pleasant. Any joy that I had experienced in believing in the jolly old guy was eclipsed by the trauma of feeling deceived. Being a shy child and lacking close friends, perhaps my relationship with my parents was more pivotal than is normally the case. (As if anything is ever "normal" for a child.)

If I had talked to other children about what was happening, perhaps I could have found a broader perspective. But, as a demure and trusting child, the experience felt so large and so very unfair that it seemed it couldn't have happened to anyone ever before. Perhaps my isolation was exaggerated by the shame I felt for my parents' deceit and the loyalty I had expressed in trying to protect them.

When the big kids burst the Santa bubble at school and the truth was exposed, I had to face my parents in a different light and wondered if I could ever trust them again. It even changed my confidence in what I was told about God in Sunday school. And it changed my sense of self. Because I was no longer a "Santa believer," I no longer had an important role in the story, as the attention shifted to my little brother who was just reaching the age of becoming a believer. It provided reason for my feeling small and invisible when my parents, uncomfortable in the situation and not knowing the extent of my wounds (or having a clue as to how to repair them), looked away.

This became *my story* for far too long. My attention *to* and identification *with* this story continued to play itself out—even into my adult life. I played the victim and complained of my invisibility to anyone close to me. I had been, however, growing tired of myself—and this old story. Telling it in this book, and looking at it again and again, I began to despise its whiney nature.

At some point, with all my emphasis on imagination as expressed in previous pages, I realized that I could look at my old story again from a different angle—perhaps even several angles—and see it in a different light that felt better. To the extent that it felt like I was "making up" any of those revised perspectives, it also suddenly felt as though I had "made up" the tragic perspective to which I had clung for so much of my life. I realized that *any* personal perspective is the absolute creation of the individual who holds it. With that revelation, the totality of my past memories seemed to actually change as if they were transmuted by a rite of passage.

As the memory healed, all accompanying upset was diffused. It no longer had the power to hurt me. It was no longer a story that, in its telling, evoked unpleasant feelings. It was just a series of events or "what happened then," which was not as important as what happened later when I learned how to see it anew, and the eternally "what is happening now." After all, the experience I had as a child was the result of *how I saw it.* When I learned to see it differently, it could not remain the same story. Its effects on me changed so thoroughly that it was as though I had gone back in time and rewritten the experience.

OLD GHOST STORIES

You're probably familiar with the book or various movie renditions of Charles Dickens' classic tale, *A Christmas Carol.* At the beginning of the story, the character of Scrooge serves as an archetype, the epitome of greed and misery—the antithesis of Santa. However, as the story unfolds, Scrooge is taken on a journey and reviews his life from the vantage of past, present, and future. He sees the events of his past and realizes that it was his *response* to these events that made him who he currently was. When he sees his current perspectives and beliefs and choices played out in the future, he sees only increased isolation and despair.

Making a choice to use this new-found worldview as a catalyst, Scrooge makes changes in his life attitudes and is inspired to take action, which begins to undo the effects of his past and transform his present and future forever. Clearly, the contrast between his previously dour perception of life and its miserly effects lead him to blossom into the joyful, generous, and Santa-like character at the end of the tale. Despite the happy ending and the genuinely transformed man, to this day the name "Scrooge" is usually presented as a symbol of a selfish and wretched man, who hurls "bah humbug" to all within earshot.

When we look at the text, it seems clear that Dickens would prefer us to remember the transformed man. He wrote that Scrooge became a second father to Tiny Tim and a benefactor to the town and "… it became said of him that he knew how to keep Christmas well, if any man alive possessed the knowledge." Scrooge had a Santa transformation—he became jolly and generous and beloved.

Is it possible that we enjoy the drama and the struggle of good and evil so much that we have immortalized the struggle itself? Have we overlooked the simplest and sweetest of lessons shown us by the shift in perception of one man? Ebenezer Scrooge changed his world and the world of those around him by letting go of his painful past and transmuting his present situation.

Looking back in my own life, I feel now that holding on to the story of a painful past took a lot more effort than letting go did. However, I must admit that "letting go" did require some adjustments on my part. I had to open myself to allow in some new ideas and revelations about the past that my old Santa story was hiding. By devising a new Santa story for my "child-self," I experienced a transformation in my life and a healing of old memories. This is how it unfolded for me. First, I had a realization about the way my parents played Santa with me.

My parents, Andy and Ruth Trahan, with my daughters, Janine and Alexa. This was the year Janine first showed me she could "play Santa" as Santa. My visiting parents experienced the joy of Santa and were blissfully unaware of the expanded story that my children and I celebrated.

NEW STORIES FOR OLD SANTAS

In the realm of my own unhappy Santa memories, I do not feel that my parents intended any malice. They were my parents. They loved me. How could they be anything but innocent in that love?

Having experienced my own children's impressionable years as a parent, I know that each moment is simply what it is. When my children look at what I did during any given situation in their childhood, I would like them to be able to shrug and say, "Well, it was the best she could do at the time." The first step in my healing was to see that my parents were not the enemy or even the cause of my pain. They were, however, integral players in my Santa story.

My parents raised me with very exact ideas about truth. Stretching the truth was a lie. "Telling a story" was a sin. So did they ever consider their Santa construct to be a bunch of untruths—and then consciously decide to lie to me? I truly doubt it. Instead, I expect that they were caught up in the momentum of the holiday and had the time of their lives creating what they believed to be a magical experience for my younger brother and me.

I suspect that they wanted their children to have the playful experience with Santa that they had missed out on. I don't for a minute think they intentionally deceived us. In fact, I don't think they thought about it at all. Ever. Likely they were also clueless to my reactions, which, after all, I kept hidden from them. They were busy taking care of themselves, doing what made them happy while wishing to share the joy. They played in the Santa construct with abandon and probably expected everyone else to enjoy it as much as they did.

They *played* in a grand way with me all through my youth. Boating, camping, water-skiing, picnics, family vacations, go-carts—all were a part of my growing up experience. Other than an occasional game of cards with the neighbors, it seemed that my parents were always playing with us children. As a child of the Depression, my dad was very young when he took on adult responsibilities, including a full-time job. As a parent, I suspect he was, for the first time, able to engage in child-like playing to an extent that his own childhood didn't allow.

I remember one year when Dad jumped into the Halloween spirit and built an elaborate House of Horror in our garage for a party. My whole class and all the neighbors were invited. I organized the line of children who walked, one at a time, into the House of Horror. What appeared to be a stuffed giant doll in a casket was really my dad. The "body" would suddenly moan and reach for the partygoer, always eliciting a scream. It was so effective that it worked every time. Dad loved it, and I was proud of hosting the best party EVER.

So here were my parents, playing with us kids and throwing the best Santa experience ever for us, year after year, using their imaginations to brighten each moment. In fact, it was eventually one of these imaginative choices that helped me connect the dots as to *who* Santa really was.

My first clue to the discovery of them being Santa was my observation that the presents from family and friends were wrapped in festive seasonal paper, but the presents from Santa were arranged under the tree without wrapping paper. This was different from the way Santa delivered presents at other houses. Maybe my parents got the idea to do this from images of Santa pulling toys out of his sack minus wrappings. Perhaps it was an attempt to duplicate a toy store window display, bright and alluring, and full to the brim.

What my parents created for me from Santa was a thrill. To walk into the room on Christmas morning and see all the presents carefully arranged was mesmerizing. I would just stand and look, seeing first one thing and then another. My gaze would travel in amazement, taking it all in. I took my time appreciating each present, commenting and pointing, and then adjusting my position to see more. If I hadn't acknowledged a particular item, perhaps overlooked, Mom or Dad would point it out to me. Everything stayed just as it was for a long golden moment, perfect and waiting and beautiful, while I surveyed the entire scene and gloried in each and every gift, and the astonishing abundance of them all together.

In another family dynamic there might have been chaos; in fact, I do recall that my younger-by-six-years brother approached Santa's bounty quite differently. He would go to the first thing he saw and immediately engage in playing with it. This would continue until something else caught his eye and he moved on. We each had our style.

As I was writing a previous chapter in this book and describing the Christmas morning tableau of unwrapped presents under the tree, I had a mental image of both of my parents as children, noses pressed against a store's front window. They were gazing at a magnificent display of toys that they would never own—because Santa never came to either of their homes. I was moved.

I am moved again as I write this. How glad I am that they knew financial security as adults. How wonderful it is that they managed to create such abundant displays of gifts for their children. How thrilling it must have been for them to be in the position to *be* the Santa that they had never known.

NEW VIEWS OF SANTA

I wondered if this time-travel vision of my parents as small children looking into the store window was my own invention, or if I had remembered a long-ago story that one of them had told me. My mother has passed and I have not spoken to my dad about it. However, whether based in fact or simply birthed by my imagination, that image, which came to me unsolicited, has softened my view about the Santa of my youth. I came to realize that I had used my parents' attempts to provide a magnificent Christmas as an excuse to carry the mantle of victimhood. Their objective had not been to trick or deceive me.

By simply viewing my childhood Santa experience with new eyes, I have now transformed the story and my own history. And here's an accompanying wonder! In this new history, I now see my young self in a new way—as a part of a wonderful game my parents played for themselves as much as for me. My part had been simply to let them play it. The rest doesn't matter so much anymore. Indeed it seems now to be petty. It has become more and more of a reach to recall the feeling of victimhood, and I am *only* interested in doing so if it serves others to know that they, too, can let go of old memories that no longer serve them.

Considering the incredible amount of peace it brought me, it's interesting that the story that became my catalyst—at least initially—was about my parents' Santa experience, not my own. By imagining my parents' Santa experience in this way and creating my own "story" about their childhoods, I had a new idea of their motivations. And that new perspective changed my reaction. As Epictetus said, "It is not what happens to you, but how you react to it that matters."

This decision to "revisit" Santas past in our lives doesn't have to be traumatic. If you decide to take the plunge, I suggest doing so without a big agenda. Rather than pursuing an outcome that you've predetermined, let a new vision come to you. Use your imagination in seeing the story from different angles. Be easy with it. This process is not about forgiveness (even if forgiveness results from it) and it's not about excuses. It's just a bridge. It is an investigation and an allowing, and something will reveal itself in the story. There will be a crack through which the light shines and a connection is made. You need only be willing.

SANTA KEEPS ON GIVING

This new Santa story that came to me spontaneously was sufficient for me to remap my past experience. And then, perhaps as a result of giving my old Santa story permission to bare its previously hidden secrets, an even bigger gift unfolded

—an even deeper insight into what I now know as my "Santa rite of passage."

Earlier in this book I referred to the exchange with my mother that was to become another "connecting-the-dots" revelation. When I first asked her, "Is Santa real?" she turned away from me, likely to mask her own uncertainty about how to handle the situation, or perhaps simply in a spontaneous attempt to avoid it altogether. She just didn't respond. How could she know how this devastated me; how disenfranchised I felt?

At the time I interpreted it to mean that I was no longer the center of her world. I had fallen from grace, no longer believing that whatever she told me must be true. I was suddenly faithless, and my faithlessness had cost me the affection I doted on.

If it seems that I am over dramatizing this, I'm not doing so for effect. It was truly a traumatic experience for me. Not because my mother called for it, deserved it, or created it, but because that is the way my young eyes saw it. I was without anchor, drifting and lost. I no longer knew what was true. I had no beliefs that I could continue to trust and I was no longer safely within my mother's constant gaze.

This singular moment of "becoming invisible" became a recurring theme for upset—many, many times in my life, with various casts of characters. How dare anyone treat me as invisible—especially my immediate family! Any time I felt ignored, or marginalized, or simply treated as a bystander— when I really wanted to be in the thick of things—I played this victim card with great drama. Being unseen felt like the deepest cruelty, for it was completely disempowering. I was a walking player in a real-life nightmare in which I scream and no sound comes out.

So, like everyone, I compensated for my insecurities the best I knew how. I lived to be important in the eyes of those important to me but was unable to fully achieve the acknowledgement I so diligently sought. In writing this I have to smile at all the high drama in this. *I challenge you to acquire a wound more deep or serviceable than mine!* What a relief to call it "past."

I recently learned from a wise friend that when we let our children know that they are not the center of our universe, it is an empowering gift. When I first heard this I thought about how kids seem to call for assurance from their parents all the time: *"Look, Mom. Watch while I do this trick. Are you watching?"* Of course, when children are infants the attention that they require can make it seem that an entire universe does indeed revolve around them. As I pondered all this, I considered the wisdom of the gradual distancing of the child from the parent until ... Wait! Was my mother doing me a *favor* when she turned away? *Breathe, Arita, breathe.* She was.

Somewhere deep inside me a bell began to toll. Ah-ha! As a child, I had felt a physical sensation of falling in that moment of separation, felt the foundation of my world fall away. Like the babe in the cradle falling from the tree, the wind had blown and I had been dropped into a new paradigm where I was the center of my own universe. I was **autonomous**. I was not prepared for it and yet there it was.

This new worldview was created there for me—actually, somehow *by* me—and it was the beginning of a totally new life journey. It was the liberty bell I was hearing. I had been handed my freedom from dependence on my parents. They ceased being gods to me in that instant. They became simply human.

Now, having been delivered from dependence did not mean that it wasn't going to take me time to grow into my independence. In the lifetime it took Moses and his people to cross from bondage into the Promised Land, crossing the Red Sea was only the beginning of the journey. When those people found themselves cut off from their Egyptian masters they didn't celebrate. In fact, they complained that they had eaten better before they left.

Indeed, my time of increased independence didn't feel like a time for celebration, either. There was no one else I could depend on to tell me what to believe and who to believe. I was bereft. It took me years to realize that in any instance, with anyone, at any time, the only person who can guarantee my presence, my power, my value, is me. Dependence on that from anyone else is futile. Knowing this now to be true, I can credit that uncomfortable, earth-quaking, and awakening moment in the kitchen with my mother as a rite of passage into my own personhood.

How wonderful it would be if we, as a culture, could acknowledge that rebirth into autonomy and celebrate ourselves and our children through the pains of passage. I had felt and continued to feel loved by my parents, in every possible way they understood. That love could not preclude my need, at that young age, to begin assuming responsibility for loving myself.

132

Obviously my ability to do this was in its infancy, but where else can anything begin?

I am appreciating my understanding of this concept as it continues to expand (like the universe) on a daily basis. *I - am - the - center - of - my - universe.* Now that I am conscious of that, I am eager for all those I love to know themselves as the center of their own universe. How much less complicated and more powerful the individual life now appears to me. Welcome to my new world! In this worldview, I tend to myself and make choices for myself, because I love and value myself so completely. Who could do it better? I require less of others and am therefore in a position to appreciate all that they do offer so much more.

I may not have been groomed for this kind of empowerment, and may have waited late in life to recognize its development, but that makes it seem all the sweeter. Just like other crash and burn moments I have experienced, I have risen like the phoenix into a greater expression of myself. Like Scrooge, it is good. I am grateful for those moments of reconstruction, of recreation, of rebirth.

YOUR SANTA GHOSTS

These insights are a direct result of my Santa experience so many years ago, revisiting it and inquiring of it. First I allowed for a new vision and interpretation of the scene as it involved all the players. As I recalled the beauty of that scene, of Santa's display under the tree, a different image revealed itself as I saw it through my parents' eyes as children themselves. From that perspective, I was newly able to acknowledge and appreciate my own awkward segue from naïve babe to open-eyed youth, as something to celebrate.

I encourage you to delve into your old Santa stories and explore a fresh approach to them. The ghosts of Santas past will likely serve you, just as they did Scrooge—and me. Our present experience is the cumulative result of stories told again and again. Change the story, change the present, direct your future. Santa is your gift to yourself to tell and retell any way you wish.

CHAPTER 7

SANTA AS A RITE OF PASSAGE
AWAKING FROM INNOCENCE

As adults, how often have we looked back on the events of our lives and recognized how pivotal some were? Sometimes in retrospect, we see that even seemingly insignificant events, as well as the traumatic ones, became turning points in our lives. I find that age has a way of assisting in this recognition, as the perspective we gain with distance often brings clarity. Many times events in my life that seemed horrible contributed to highly desirable outcomes.

SANTA AS LIFE MARKER

When I consider my own turning points, those events that served to reinvent me, I see that they also serve as markers on the journey into whom I have become. Our crises (painful or not) are like chapter titles in the story of our lives. Prior to each life-changing event, we might have considered ourselves to be one thing, and after the event something else altogether.

I don't know about yours, but many of those early pivotal moments in my life were not at all comfortable. At the time, the discomfort I felt made me wish for a change in the *circumstances*. Now, in retrospect, I can see that what was really called for was a change in *me*. With each crisis, the shift in awareness that came from moving through the change allowed me to participate in the development of a future full of more pleasurable moments. It's as though the rough ride had to precede the smooth one, and certainly allowed me to appreciate it more.

Mike's story encapsulates the rite of passage that the outing of Santa is to many:

> *I vividly recall standing at the urinal in the boy's restroom at school and overhearing other boys talking about how there really wasn't a Santa. They said that their parents were Santa. I was shocked. I'll never forget that moment standing there. And then after that, after I no longer believed, there just weren't as many presents. Did you ever notice that? I remember thinking, "What else have they told me that isn't true?"*
>
> *(Mike)*

Mike told me the last part of the story above several times. He wanted me to get it right. It hadn't been fun.

I think it is appropriate to consider these crises as rites of passage, even though we didn't enter into them with that consciousness. Perhaps the most valuable rite of passage is always entered unawares, and valued only after our survival of it. When we look back at them this way we can see the good on both sides of the moment with the event itself serving as the turning-point, the point of change.

PINOCCHIO ARCHETYPE

The construct that the current culture has created for Santa reminds me of Geppetto and Pinocchio. When we deceive, we are caught in that legendary web where noses grow—and stories get out of control. In the Santa story, both parent and child take turns playing roles as puppet and puppeteer.

As parents, we play the puppeteer when we educate our children in their roles in the construct of Santa. Our children dance along to the story as we guide them. Later, when children pretend along with the story long after they know the truth, the roles reverse and they are the ones pulling the strings as they watch their parents dance around their questions.

At that point, our children have become more like us than we might have wished. They take their turn manipulating us— the child now the wiser—and the parent the one who is being deceived. When the truth is openly acknowledged by both child and parent, then love and forgiveness transform our wooden natures into flesh and blood, and we are all real again. The fallibility we have demonstrated in our dishonesty makes us vulnerable, as we have never been before. We are no longer gods to our children. We are, however, human, and that's a good thing.

The timing of Santa is perfect for a rite of passage. The Santa story begins at an age when we are at our most impressionable and most capable of living fully in a world of magic. It culminates as we are entering a world of factuality and autonomy, one of the numerous steps we take in distancing ourselves from our parents in the healthy way that leads eventually to maturity and the ability to live life as individuals.

The pivotal point within the Santa story is the awakening of any child to the "truth" about Santa. The crisis doesn't have to be painful—though it sometimes is. No one can choose how our children feel but them. And even if it is painful, that doesn't negate the beneficial aspects of the rite. We do what feels best and right to us as their parents and their response is theirs to make.

No matter how honestly or gently you might present Santa, there is always the possibility that the child may resent that Santa is not what they want him to be. Regardless, the journey itself is a good one, and one that can serve both parent and child in the process.

The timing of Santa in our lives *as parents* is also perfect for a rite of passage. Up until this point in our parenting we have felt god-like in our power and ability to navigate our children through their experiences. We choose everything for them in the beginning—where and when and what and why. We are masters of their fate—or so it may seem.

When we are playing a Santa who "knows when you are sleeping" and "knows when you're awake," we can feel omniscient and omnipresent. It's easy to buy into the idea because it feels all-powerful and, at the same time, benevolent. Then we are found out. First we are master manipulators; then we lose control of the strings … and *our children*! Yikes.

Suddenly we are observed as contriving and deceiving by these young, previously innocent children, and the discovery can feel like a loss of dignity. The beautiful thing here is that there always comes a time for us, as parents, to fail in our ability to control the lives of our children. To do it grandly, and often without complete recovery of that integrity, can actually assist us in recognizing our children as individuals well on their way to the complete and competent lives of their own. They have their own abilities to discern and believe as they wish. *Back away from the children*. They are more powerful than you might have thought.

If you have already taught your children to believe in Santa and you have picked up this book because you aren't sure how to get them from that awkward stage—going from "believing" to no longer believing—then here's how the transition can become something to celebrate—for both of you.

A child's questioning is to be expected and to be appreciated—something that we want to encourage in their lives "out there" in the world as well as within the family. We may feel disheartened that the period of naiveté has past and the storytelling has changed, but it can still be fun for both parties.

We can't keep our children babies forever. Embrace their growth along with your own. We can elevate the revelation, the discovery that there is no actual Santa, from something that is horrifying or embarrassing to something that is enlightening. It can be honored.

If there are fewer presents, it's because we've grown into present-giving more than present-receiving. Learning to "play Santa" with your child introduces giving anonymously, which is the most fun part of all. The truth about Santa is now made sacred; this elevates it into a rite of passage.

WIZARD OF OZ ARCHETYPE

Over and over we were told by parents that they engaged in the cultural Santa construct to protect the child's innocence and their belief in magic. We are conflicted regarding our children. We want keep them babies, even though this effort is obviously doomed for failure. Since the end is always the same—predictable discovery and growth—and because we cannot expect otherwise, on some level we want that part, too.

By putting ourselves in charge of the magic, we operate behind a curtain like the Wizard of Oz. Ultimately, our need to fabricate the magic is also our undoing. We have led our children down the yellow brick road and, just as the Wizard's flashing lights provided "evidence" of his power to create magic, so too, we have been providing evidence of our Santa construct. And, like the Wizard, by doing so, we have failed to recognize our children's ability to create magic by themselves all along the journey. With each turn in the road there is risk and recovery, and along the way there are lessons in courage and love and intelligence. The Wizard may require the journey and designate the path, but the journey is one they take on their own.

Now it's time to point out what has been true all along, and award those prizes like the Wizard did in Oz. Our children can know themselves as *smart* to have figured it all out, *brave* to be willing to cross over to the other side of the Santa story, and *big-hearted* to become a giver as well as a receiver.

Even though the "magic" demonstrated by the parents when they "played" Santa themselves is indeed not real, the magic within the child can remain intact. The Wizard of Oz didn't make the Cowardly Lion brave or the Scarecrow smart. He didn't give the Tin Man a heart. They already had the qualities they were seeking. Children already have the ability to believe before we insist that they do. And their way of believing in magic is more fun and safer, because there is no abrupt ending to the tale.

Yes, Dorothy and her friends could have gone home any time along the path if they'd only known that they could. But they believed in the Wizard and thought they had to take the troubled path, only to learn later that he was not what they thought. Do not despair.

Remember that it is the journey and not the destination that life is all about. Your children, too, will learn that you are not what they had thought, just as you learned that truth about your parents. You will be busted. Your powers are fake and your awards are phony unless you openly acknowledge the real gifts as belonging to the children all along. Going home to the truth of Auntie Em is still the happy ending of the story, as is finding out that you are the Wizard behind the Santa curtain. It's the right time to go home. The journey along the yellow brick road was one of revelation and growth.

There's something so seductive about the idea that our children are innocent, and we long to keep them that way. But innocence is fleeting and, in fact, must be. If your children were innocent when they began playing their role in your Santa construct, they weren't innocent in the same way when they were finished. They most likely even participated in knowing the "truth" about Santa and engaged in deceiving you into thinking they didn't.

MY OWN SANTA RITE OF PASSAGE

I can now appreciate my own childhood Santa experience as being pivotal in many ways. As an overly well-behaved child, more interested in pleasing her parents than anything else, my emotional evolution required that I find reasons to separate myself from them. Although the time to physically separate ourselves as *children* from our parents—and ourselves as *parents* from our children—is indeed a season, the seeds can be planted early in that season.

Seeds of wonder and the need to question—even seeds of distrust—can grow into a healthy harvest of personal reliance. Along the way we behave as humans, making mistakes and knowing that it is acceptable to do so, because we witness our parents make them too. We learned that it wasn't the end of the world, even if it seemed like it for a while. Thank you, Santa.

Even though I was of the generation that wore the "Question Authority" buttons, I never wore one. From my then goody-two-shoes perspective, I just stood back and marveled at the audacity of such an idea. That was too much freedom for someone like me who craved "safety" and thought that those in authority could and would provide it for me.

As I observed my own parents, it seemed to me that they were overly inclined to believe the church, the government, and their doctors, and to look to those authority figures to make decisions for them—even decisions about their own lives and bodies. Any tendency to question was quickly squelched, as they were obedient believers, citizens, and patients. This was also the choice they advised me to follow, as it was one within which they found safety.

I have come to understand that we are each at choice in every moment throughout our lives. When I notice that my Dad is relying on others to a degree that is uncomfortable for me, I have to remind myself that each person's choices are to be honored. Or, at the very least, when I see that someone else is prescribing something that I don't think is wise for my Dad, I have to be willing to shift any responsibility for a different action. I am only—and fully—in charge of my own choice-making.

143

When I was a child and I put my faith in Santa, I did not feel that was a successful investment. However, surviving the investment proved extremely valuable. I have continued believing in miracles and fantasy throughout my life. I choose where I put my faith, and I continue to discriminate and refine those choices every day. Instead of simply accepting the tenets of faith, I have enjoyed personalizing them, finding common ground with others, and appreciating diversity. I have found my place among the options, all of which I consider facets of one idea, none higher than another. Because of this selective sifting, my faith is stronger than ever before. Thank you, Santa.

I have lived with and without Santa in my life, cycling back to enjoying the jolly guy with a fresh and focused bent to the story. And it's my very own Santa story. I appreciate his presence in the midst of a cold and dark time of year, his generous nature, his playfulness, his smile, his paunchiness, his white hair, his youthfulness, and, most of all, his laughter. I relish in the story and the image of a Santa that suits me perfectly. I relish in a life and a family and a house and a career and a faith and all the other choices that suit me perfectly. I celebrate them all and celebrate them in constantly changing ways, each more fun and satisfying than the last. Thank you, Santa.

I have grown in the understanding and appreciation of my own parents and parents everywhere, including myself, because of the Santa story. Santa elicits from us a revelation of what is to us important, what is useful, and what is timely. We know each other and ourselves better because Santa is such a catalyst. Thank you, Santa.

I recognize myself as an individual, as unique as a snowflake. And each person in my midst is also a unique snowflake, autonomous and perfect. I know myself as center of my own universe, a universe within which there are other centers of other universes, and this self-centeredness empowers each of us. Through our own sense of power, we can choose to be loving and kind and generous, just like Santa. That makes *us* magnificent Santas, ready to play the Santa game in any minute during any season of the year. In that way, our selfishness in our own center is really the best thing we can do not only for ourselves, but also for others. Thank you, Santa.

I know myself capable of feeling like either a pawn within other people's stories or the author of my own. I am in each moment the one who is both *participating in* and *writing* these stories. I am constant witness to the process, my own and that of others, each of us doing what we know to do and what is working best for us in the moment. I especially appreciate those awkward moments that can unfold new "rites of passage." In a culture that is a little short of celebrated rites, I find myself jealous of the *bar mitzvahs* and *bat mitzvahs*, and of the *Quinceañeras*. I wish for more ways to celebrate the turning of the page from one chapter to another. For most young people, the best we have is the attainment of a driver's license and graduation from school as personal and social marks of empowerment. I jump to acknowledge any rite of passage that presents itself in order to help people of any age celebrate who they are and who they are becoming, and steer them in whatever direction they choose. Thank you, Santa.

Santa can be a stepping stone to celebrate your own rite-of-passage and new worldview to make you stronger, sweeter, more sensitive, more aware, more honest, more imaginative, more empowered to choose for yourself, more eager for change, more awake, more free, more yourself.

Thank you, Santa.

Ho, ho, ho!

ABOUT THE AUTHORS

Arita Trahan is mother, grandmother, actress, acting coach, and personal communication coach. She was born in New Orleans and recalls her childhood in Louisiana as a barefoot tree-climber. As a teen, she moved to Texas, and later as a young adult to Tennessee. She doesn't feel like a Southerner, and *knows* that she doesn't sound like one (does a fish feel water?). She is currently living—and feeling right at home—in *Southern* California.

Arita loves being a storyteller. Her favorite relationship with her 6-years-younger brother was her role as the sister who read to him. As a teen, she remembers lying sprawled across her bed reading a book, likely Jane Austen, and how difficult it was to get off the bed when she was called to dinner. It was as though she was pulling herself out of another world, shaking off the British heroine she had become, and straining to find herself again in her own teenage body.

Arita can untangle anything, loves to hike when someone else carries the pack, and is a type A personality who takes pride in being flexible. She is on a mission to increase the Santa joy and magic. She says, "Let Santa be your favorite story … and your favorite game."

Norma Eckroate is the coauthor of numerous books. She wrote the bestselling Dog Whisperer books with Paul Owens: *The Dog Whisperer, The Puppy Whisperer* and *The Dog Whisperer Presents Good Habits for Great Dogs*. Norma also co-authored the bestselling *The Natural Cat*, which has been called the "Bible" of natural cat care, as well as *Switched-On Living, The Natural Dog* and *Complete Holistic Care and Healing for Horses*.

In addition to writing, Norma has worked extensively in both theatre and television. Most recently, she produced Paul Owens' Dog Whisperer DVDs, *The Dog Whisperer: Beginning and Intermediate Dog Training* and *The Dog Whisperer, Vol. 2: Solving Common Behavior Problems for Puppies and Dogs*.

Norma has a B.A. in dramatic arts from Kent State University and an M.A. in metaphysical science from the University of Sedona. She is a licensed spiritual practitioner at the Agape International Spiritual Center in Culver City, California, and also teaches metaphysics and spirituality.

I'm Being Santa

Music: Mark Horwitz; Lyrics: Arita Trahan

Lyric	*What it Means*
I don't have to wear a red coat	My success isn't limited by how I dress
Or grow a long white beard	or my physical appearance
Or come down someone's chimney	or even some action journey someone else determines.
That would just be weird.	I can laugh at limitations!
When I give in secret	When I love and give unconditionally
So no one else will know	without dependence on the approval of others
It feels so-so very good,	I experience divine joy.
I have to go Ho-Ho-Ho.	And my life is evidence of that joy.

Chorus:

Ho-ho-ho, I'm being Santa,	*I love my life of giving,*
Thinking 'bout the gifts I can give	*It's fun to think of others*
To the ones I love.	*And how I can add to their lives.*
Ho-ho-ho, I'm being Santa,	*I get to choose who I am*
Every day and night	*And experience my life*
'Cause it feels so right.	*As one that feels divinely good*
I'm being Santa	*By focusing my thoughts*
That's what I'm thinking of.	*Because the way I think affects my experience.*

It's all about the giving	My life is for expressing love
And not the *thank-you* part.	And not about getting approval from others.
'Cause when I give in secret	And when I give anonymously
The gift is from my heart.	It is an expression of unconditional love—divine love.
Look around—the world is full	My expression is evidence of an abundant universe
Of happy sweet surprise.	That conspires to bless and gift me.
And everywhere you turn you'll see	Everything and everyone I see in my world
There are Santas in disguise!	Is there as a blessing for me!

Chorus:

Ho-ho-ho, I'm being Santa	*I am a giver*
Thinking 'bout the gifts I can give	*Thinking about my giving*
To the ones I love.	*And about all those who can receive my gifts.*
Ho-ho-ho, I'm being Santa	*I am a giver.*
Every day and night	*It is my life*
'Cause it feels so right.	*I choose this because it is my happiest choice.*
I'm being Santa.	*I am a giver.*
That's what I'm thinking of.	*My thoughts create my life.*

I can give a gift, bright shiny and new	I can give with my money like a present
Or an act of kindness	Or I can give with my time and my energy without money.
That's something I can do!	Both are gifts, and there is *always* a way for me to give.

(Chorus)

Song available at www.TheSantaStory.com